THE
TWILIGHT
PHENOMENON

FORBIDDEN
FRUIT OR
THIRST-QUENCHING
FANTASY?

KURT BRUNER

THE
TWILIGHT
PHENOMENON

FORBIDDEN
FRUIT OR
THIRST-QUENCHING
FANTASY?

DESTINY IMAGE® PUBLISHERS, INC.

P.O. Box 310, Shippensburg, PA 17257-0310

"Speaking to the Purposes of God for This Generation and for the Generations to Come."

This book and all other Destiny Image, Revival Press, MercyPlace, Fresh Bread, Destiny Image Fiction, and Treasure House books are available at Christian bookstores and distributors worldwide.

For a U.S. bookstore nearest you, call 1-800-722-6774.

For more information on foreign distributors, call 717-532-3040.

Reach us on the Internet: www.destinyimage.com

ISBN 10: 0-7684-3136-0
ISBN 13: 978-0-7684-3136-0

For Worldwide Distribution, Printed in the U.S.A.

1 2 3 4 5 6 7 8 9 10 11 / 13 12 11 10 09

CONTENTS

ABOUT THE AUTHOR

Kurt Bruner is the best-selling author of more than a dozen books including *Finding God in the Lord of the Rings*, *Finding God in the Land of Narnia*, *Shedding Light on His Dark Materials*, and *Inklings of God*. He serves as Pastor of Spiritual Formation with Lake Pointe Church near Dallas, Texas. A former vice president with Focus on the Family, Kurt led teams creating books, magazines, films, and radio drama—including the popular *Adventures in Odyssey* and *Chronicles of Narnia* series. Find free resources for your spiritual journey at www.KurtBruner.com.

INTRODUCTION

THE TWILIGHT PHENOMENON

By the time I became aware of the *Twilight* book series, it was already a phenomenon. While shopping one day, I walked by a large display rack lined with face-out book covers; black background with hands cradling a deep-red apple. The title told me nothing of the content. I assumed it had something to do with forbidden fruit.

"It doesn't seem good to me," the store clerk volunteered.

"What doesn't seem good?"

"All of these teenage girls reading a book about falling in love with a vampire," he said. "But it sure is popular!"

He had no idea. Number one *New York Times*

bestseller turned blockbuster film that put vampire posters on prominent display in adolescent bed-rooms and lockers. And closer to home, the near obsession of "all but one girl" in my fifth-grade son's elementary classroom.

I soon discovered that Stephenie Meyer had created an entire series of titles in which the main story line is a teenage girl falling passionately in love with a 100-year-old vampire who, according to the fans, is "hot."

On the surface of things I could understand the clerk expressing concern about *Twilight's* popularity. But then I encountered girls, moms, and a few guys who couldn't get enough. Even many conservative Christian parents seemed untroubled that their teenage girls were devouring books that merge adolescent crush with blood-lust. I simply had to find out for myself what was so appealing about the series. So, pushing aside a stack of "must read" titles sitting beside my bed, I dove into Meyer's world—eventually reading all four titles—*Twilight, New Moon, Eclipse,* and *Breaking Dawn.*

I had a similar experience about a decade earlier when my then 8-year-old son came home from school begging me to buy him a new book called *Harry Potter and the Sorcerer's Stone.*

"I don't see why not." I began. News stories were calling *Harry Potter* the best thing to hit publishing since the Gutenberg press because, miracle of miracle, it was getting boys excited about reading. But popular doesn't always mean good, so my wife gave me "the look" from across the room. I knew I better hit the pause button so the two of us could conspire.

"I've heard about that book from other parents," she whispered "and think it would be a good idea for you to read it first. They say it's promoting witchcraft."

Yikes! It didn't sound like the best selection for an impressionable boy. So I made a deal with Kyle. "I will read it first and then, if I think it's OK, we will read the book together so that we can discuss the themes."

Like millions of others I got pulled into the wonders of Hogwarts School of Witchcraft and Wizardry and the drama of Harry discovering his hidden powers and unexpected destiny. Years later, Kyle has read all seven Harry Potter titles and has not—as some feared—left the Christian faith for dark-magic or the Wicca cult. In retrospect, the paranoia of some over the Harry Potter phenomenon seems a bit silly—largely founded on a misunderstanding of the nature of fantasy literature. But in this day and age I prefer parents who are overly cautious than not cautious enough about the media their children consume. There is a lot of really bad stuff out there.

Some have said that the *Twilight* phenomenon among girls is similar to what the Harry Potter craze was for boys; a harmless fantasy series they can enjoy with little fear of negative influence. Others view it with more suspicion, concerned the themes introduced feel somehow inappropriate for young readers. This book exists to help fans and critics alike reflect upon many of the profoundly important ideas raised by the *Twilight* phenomenon, including deeply spiritual concepts such as:

- what it means to be human,

- the nature of the soul, and

- how romantic love inspires us toward our ultimate destiny.

I am not the first to provide commentary on spiritual themes in Stephenie Meyer's work, nor will I be the last. Even *Time* magazine noted that the author's religious perspective heavily influenced her storytelling, going so far as to suggest that her beliefs are key to understanding her books—making special note that being an "observant Mormon" who "doesn't drink alcohol and has never seen an R-rated movie"[1] played a part in the personality of the stories; a trite way of hinting at the more important recognition that spiritual themes do indeed pervade the world and worries of key characters like Bella Swan and Edward Cullen.

For those who find the *Twilight* phenomenon suspect, I ask you to reserve judgment as we dive into ideas that—at the very least—will shed light on what would make such dark themes so appealing.

If you are a *Twilight* fan I ask you to experience the books and films with spiritual eyes. Many of your favorite scenes and story lines are probably rooted in realities more important than you realize.

SPIRITUAL FORMATION

Why did I write this book? First because I am a Spiritual Formation Pastor, which means I spend most of my time helping people take next steps on their spiritual journey. I believe that journey has a specific path and destination. My Christian faith teaches that we were made "in the image and likeness of God" with tremendous potential for goodness, beauty, love, joy, and life. That's the good news. The bad news is that the human race is fallen, so we easily roll downhill toward things we were never intended to experience, like evil, corruption, hatred, misery, and death. Spiritual formation is about climbing uphill rather than tumbling down it by becoming more and more like our Lord and Savior Jesus Christ.

The second reason I wrote this book is because, believe it or not, fantasy literature and blockbuster films can aid in that spiritual climb. How? By confronting us with deeply spiritual questions raised, intentionally or not, in the plot and characters presented. As we will explore, the author of *Twilight* follows a long line of writers who have carried readers into fantasy worlds in ways that awaken both troubling and inspiring real-world concerns. Myths and legends gave the ancients a common vocabulary for grappling with spiritual realities. Ghost stories caused medieval townsfolk to avoid dark superstitions. Grimm's Fairy Tales gave generations of young children a moral compass for proper behavior. Scholars like George MacDonald, J.R.R. Tolkien, and C.S. Lewis created fantasy novels laced with profound Christian truths about the nature of good and evil. And modern storytellers like Madam L'Engle, J.K. Rowling, and Philip

Pullman have created other worlds that intentionally mirror the moral and spiritual conflicts of our own. In like manner, Stephenie Meyer is one of many vampire love story authors who have created fantasy-world stories through which we can encounter real-world questions.

One of the most important vehicles of our spiritual formation is the imagination. God gave humankind a hunger for inventing and hearing stories. No child can resist curling up beside Mom or Dad to hear the next chapter of a wonderful book. Something magical happens when those four words "Once upon a time" carry us into strange lands and unknown adventures. Boys, girls, men, and women alike love stories because we are all hungry to connect with reality. That's right, I said *connect* with reality—not escape reality. Fictional tales, perhaps more than any other form of storytelling, bring us face to face with the most important realities in all of life. Stephenie Meyer has done nothing particularly new. She stands in good company for good reason.

What may seem unique is how the *Twilight* phenomenon marries two traditionally distinct story genres: romance and gothic horror. Meyer's books are by no means the first to bring the two together, but they have certainly been the most successful if book and t-shirt sales are any indication. *Twilight's* success has even spawned an industry of copy-cat stories and brought formerly dead vampire books out of publisher coffins. Not long ago you would have received a blank stare if you asked a bookstore clerk to point you to the vampire romance section. Now you may have difficulty locating any other section due to the enormous popularity of books trying to quench our thirst for bloodcurdling love.

How do such stories influence our spiritual formation? That depends upon two things. First, the author's underlying assumptions and philosophy. Every writer champions some sort of spiritual agenda whether they realize it or not. What we create draws upon a deep well of personal experiences, beliefs, and values. Most of us don't even realize the ways in which we've been shaped by our parents and siblings, religious and academic instruction, books we've read, friends we've known, media we've consumed, and feelings we've felt. We carry all of these influences with us into the creative process and they bubble up onto the page whether we want them to or not. That's why we will attempt to decipher key ideas the author's work advances, whether she intended to or not.

Another factor in how a story affects our

spiritual formation is the lenses through which we read. Each of us carries our own assumptions, attitudes, and influences into the experience of reading or watching a story unfold. My second son, for example, reacts with angry indignation to any villain abusing an innocent victim. His emotional reaction has been, at least in part, sparked by memories of being bullied by a fourth-grade classmate. He does not read the book consciously looking for villains to hate. He just happens to hate the ones who appear. The same thing occurs when it comes to our spiritual perspective. That's why it is important to reflect upon every story we read using the "lenses" of Christian teachings. We want to make sure to benefit from the good stuff and properly discern the bad. Remember, just because something tastes good does not make it good for you.

But reading through the lenses of Christian teaching can be tricky. We don't want to dissect a story before we've allowed ourselves to experience it. Fantasy tales are meals to be enjoyed, not homework to be endured. So while I may provide a summary of key themes and scenes from the *Twilight* series, I do so assuming readers have or will read the full novels. For those who have yet to read the books, I hope to answer some of the questions posed by their popularity.

POSING QUESTIONS

Many who have observed the *Twilight* phenomenon are scratching their heads and wondering "What's up with that?" A very good question that deserves thoughtful response. So do several other questions raised by rabid fans and leery parents alike, including:

- Is it OK for teen (and preteen) girls to read a series about forbidden love with a dangerous "boy"?

- Why are we so fascinated with dark characters like vampires, and what does that fascination suggest about our own nature?

- What are vampires? Do they have souls?

- What is the relationship between romantic attraction and true love?

- What sacrifices can or should we make for love?

- Are we defined by our nature or our choices?

- What is immortality and how is it lost? How is it gained?

- How do we discern between good desire and bad temptation?

- What is the nature of evil?

- What does it mean to be heroic?

- Is the emergence of the *Twilight* phenomenon essentially good or basically evil?

These are some of the questions I hope to address in the following pages. Before we dive in, however, I want to give you a quick overview of the road ahead.

In the first three chapters we will take a look at the genre of fantasy literature as a whole and vampire stories in particular. We often read too much or too little into a story because we misunderstand the "rules" that govern such tales. We will also explore the power of human imagination and how stories of this nature can move us either up or downhill.

In Chapters Four and Five we will explore the meaning and purpose of romantic love including the good we need, the bad we crave, and the reality we yearn to know. As we will discover, Bella's love interests suggest a great deal about our own love hunger. In the last chapter we will discuss another important theme that emerges throughout the *Twilight* series—the reality and destiny of the soul.

I hope this book helps you turn our cultural obsession with vampire romance into a personal journey of spiritual growth.

Chapter One

The Power of Stories

*Edward had always thought that he belonged to the world of horror stories. Of course, I'd known he was dead wrong. It was obvious that he belonged **here**. In a fairy tale.*[1] —Bella Swan

So, what's the big deal? After all, these are just fictional stories. Why so much hype and holler over a series of romance novels?

Why indeed.

To understand the Twilight Phenomenon, we must first think about the power of stories. Good stories do more than entertain us. They encourage us, challenge us, or even transform us. A well-told tale can prompt a smile, draw a tear, inspire hope, or arouse despair. It can also ignite the flame of passion and stir the desire for lasting love. That's why we can't resist curling up in that favorite chair with a good book, enjoying a large bucket of buttered popcorn while watching the latest big screen movie hit, or sitting around the table with friends and loved ones as they tell tales of days past.

Whatever form they take, we are drawn to stories like nothing else in life. We cheer when the hero on the side of right overtakes the villain on the side of wrong. Our hearts rejoice when the guy finally gets the girl and they begin their happily ever after. Despair turns to cheering as the cavalry rides in at the darkest possible moment to save the day.

I grew up attending churches that placed a high priority on expository Bible teaching. Each Sunday the pastor would take his place behind the pulpit and invite the congregation to "Open your Bibles to..." whatever passage was his main sermon text. That was our cue that we could expect the next thirty to forty minutes to include three points, a poem, two application lessons, four yawns, a few glances at the watch or PDA, and the unspoken but all important question—"*When* will this end?" The problem is not the teaching itself. The problem is that we become easily bored.

Contrast this reality with what happens when you hear the phrase "Once upon a time..." Rather than points, a poem, and "When will it end?" you expect adventure, conflict, good guys, bad guys, and romance. Some stories draw a smile, others a tear. But they always hold our attention with the unspoken but all-important question—"*How* will this end?"

The late broadcasting legend, Paul Harvey, reflecting upon the power of art over argument penned these words:

> *Nobody could have persuaded a generation of Americans to produce a baby boom—yet Shirley Temple movies made every couple want to have one. Military enlistments were lagging for our Air Force until, almost overnight, a movie called "Top Gun" had recruits standing in line. The power of art over argument.[2]*

Harvey goes on to explain how several great books of the 19th century had a dramatic impact upon their time. For example, British sweatshops for children thrived until Charles Dickens wrote about them—turning public sentiment. American slavery ended only after Harriet Beecher Stowe's book *Uncle Tom's Cabin* sold hundreds of thousands of copies—giving the struggling abolitionist movement the attention and support it needed. Even Abraham Lincoln gave her credit for having started the Civil War. The classic *Black Beauty* led to statutes requiring more humane treatment of draft-horses. And, in another instance in which animal activists struggled to make people relate to animals...

> *Once upon a time, a cartoonist named Walt Disney created an animal character called "Bambi" and, in one year, deer hunting nose-dived from a $5.7 million business—to $1 million. The power of art over argument.*[3]

Is it any wonder that New York and Hollywood are having such an enormous impact upon our generation? It is much easier to hold the attention of a culture with "once upon a time" than with didactic teaching. And yet, the Bible itself is the ultimate "once upon a time" story filled with plots, subplots, and the dramatic themes only faintly captured on the stage or the silver screen. The twists and turns reflected in the Gospel are far more compelling than any novel ever to appear on the *New York Times* best-seller list. But we ignore the main plot while examining the mini principles, missing the forest for the trees.

HAPPILY EVER AFTER...

Have you ever wondered why, when so much of real life seems unhappy, we love happy endings? We carry with us into every story a certain expectancy that, if not satisfied, makes us feel cheated. Every "once upon a time" builds anticipation for the eventual "happily ever after." Each evil villain set upon destruction requires a virtuous hero committed to justice. A story that fails to fulfill these expectations is like an unresolved musical cord—leaving us tense, distressed, yearning for resolution.

Some would say this is because we are hopeless romantics, desiring what cannot be possessed, seeking momentary escape from the harsh realities of life. Perhaps they are right. But maybe, just maybe, there is a more compelling explanation— one which captures the imagination instead of insults it. As J.R.R. Tolkien put it, "Why should a man be scorned, if, finding himself in prison, he tries to get out and go home?"[4] What if, rather than trying to escape reality, our spirits are trying to connect with it?

What if good stories were good, not because they distract our troubled hearts, but because they affirm our deepest aspirations? Aspirations which, if allowed to flourish, would connect us to a larger story—a story within which we all play a part—a story which explains the meaning of life. What if the dramatic themes we love were actually a reflection of a true yet transcendent story being told on the stage of life? What if there really is a brave hero fighting the forces of evil in order to save the world from certain destruction? What if there really is a handsome prince in pursuit of his princess, trying to free her from the evil clutches of a seductive villain? What if, just when all seems lost, the hero actually will break free and save the day? What if "once upon a time" is truly progressing toward an eventual "happily ever after?" How would your own story change if you knew the plot of the larger story within which it is being told?

During the years I led the film and radio drama teams with Focus on the Family, I put myself on a self-directed course to learn all I could about what makes a great story. One of the most helpful books was written by screenplay expert Christopher Vogler. Using illustrations from dozens of films, Vogler revealed the common pattern found in some of the most popular movies ever produced—many of which I had enjoyed without really understanding why.

The idea was simple, and at the same time profound. All great stories adhere to the same basic structure. When that structure is followed, a story inspires people. When ignored, it bores them. These common structural elements found universally in myths, fairy tales, fables, novels, and movies are known collectively as "The Hero's Journey."

What is the hero's journey? Put simply, it is the quest pursued by the central character of every story—be it Dorothy in the *Wizard of Oz*, Christian in *Pilgrim's Progress*, or Luke Skywalker in *Star Wars*. The same pattern of overcoming obstacles in pursuit of a desired object is present in Tolkien's *The Lord of the Rings* that is found in Disney's *Toy Story*. The heroic drives that motivate young Peter in Narnia also stir King Arthur in Camelot. The settings, challenges, characters, and details are as different as can be. But the journey is the same.

Despite the infinite varieties, every story starts with a hero, or central character, living the familiar circumstances of whatever "ordinary life" he may know. But then, something happens to throw life out of balance, calling the hero onto a quest for some "object of desire." Overcoming many obstacles and challenges in pursuit of that object, there eventually comes an "ultimate confrontation" necessary to regain equilibrium to his life or world. In most cases, the stakes continue to rise until the hero faces off with some supreme antagonist—up to and often including death itself. If the hero is willing to sacrifice something precious, perhaps his or her very life, he or she can obtain the remedy needed for returning his world to a state of harmony.

One example of this pattern is the classic "guy meets girl" story evident throughout the *Twilight* series. The hero (such as Edward) is perfectly content with his life until he encounters an object of desire (Bella). Suddenly, "ordinary life" is no longer good enough. He is propelled into a quest, driven to face and overcome whatever obstacles necessary to get the girl. Ultimately, he must "die" to self-centered solitude if he hopes to win her heart and resurrect harmony to his life.

Another example is the action-adventure story. The hero is living the "ordinary life" of crime fighter, soldier, or secret agent when an ominous villain enters the picture—perhaps his old nemesis. Before you know it, the hero may be risking his life in order to save the world from certain destruction or save his beloved from an ugly bad guy. He "dies" to self-preservation in order to defeat the villain's threat. Sometimes he is literally killed, other times he is merely injured or misunderstood. But he always gives up something (life, limb, or reputation) in order to win the day.

As we will see, both the "guy meets girl" and "action-adventure" story lines surface throughout the *Twilight* series, which is a big part of why they have become so popular. We will also discover striking parallels between these themes and Christian Gospel. A hero (Christ) leaves His ordinary world (Heaven) on a quest to face His old nemesis (satan) in order to rescue an object of desire (humanity). Overcoming great obstacles, He eventually faces death to remedy the world.

If a story does not follow the pattern of the hero's journey, it fails to connect with our spirits. We bring unconscious expectations into every "once upon a time" that must be met, or we are left feeling cheated. When the story fulfills these expectations, it is like a good meal with friends. When it doesn't, we remain hungry for something else. Imagine how popular the *Star Wars* epic would have been had Luke remained home instead of fighting against the Empire. If he hadn't taken the hero's journey, there would have been no conflict, no quest, and no audience. What if Peter, Edmund, Lucy, and Susan played their game of hide and seek without entering the world of Narnia? They would never have encountered the dangers of the White Witch, the wonder of King Aslan, or any of the adventures millions have enjoyed in *The Chronicles of Narnia*.

The importance of this pattern is clear to Hollywood. Embracing the mythic power of the hero's journey enabled Walt Disney to capture the hearts (and wallets) of an entire generation. Screenplay writers and producers create box office hits each year through this classic story structure. They know that films using it will find an audience. Those that don't, won't.

Realizing that the stories we love reflect the pattern of the Christian narrative should prompt several questions. Why do all good stories follow the same basic pattern? What is the source of human yearning that makes us require the guy get the girl, the hero defeat the villain, and the underdog win the day? Could it be that deep within, on a level we may not comprehend, we are trying to connect with ultimate reality—a reality that can only be explained by and reside within a true yet transcendent story? Could it be that we yearn to know the plot to a grand drama within which our lives play a part?

While asking these questions, I came across an

interview between journalist Bill Moyers and the late Joseph Campbell, author of a book entitled *The Hero With A Thousand Faces* that inspired the concept behind the Hero's Journey. Campbell saw residing within every story, myth, legend, and fairy tale the answer to man's search for meaning in life. Though I disagreed with his clearly non-Christian perspective, I was intrigued by his findings.

Familiar with the Gospel because he had been raised in the Roman Catholic tradition, Campbell discovered the themes and patterns residing within the Christian narrative pushing their way through the myths and stories of other cultures and religions. As he discovered the similarities, he began to connect the dots. His conclusion? That all of these stories, the Christian Gospel included, reflect a deeper reality of what it means to be human. None of them, the Christian Gospel included, are necessarily true in an ultimate sense. It is what they reflect, not what they claim, that is important. Campbell placed Christ in the same category as Moses, Buddha, Mohammed, and every other religious "hero" on a "journey." Since the legend of Jesus follows the same mythic structure as every other great cultural or religious story, there must be a universal truth that all of them are trying to proclaim—but that none of them completely contain. From Campbell's perspective, they do not reflect that which is beyond us, but that which is within us.

Obviously, I couldn't agree. Christ is unique, and the Gospel is in a different category than any other story. I could not accept the notion that Jesus was just another mythic figure, or that His life, death, and resurrection were merely symbolic of every man's quest. But neither could I ignore the fact that other cultural stories, religious leaders, and heroes looked very similar to those described in the Gospel. I concluded that despite his flawed conclusion, Campbell must have encountered a piece of the truth. A truth that reinforced the existence of a universal, overarching story all others seek to tell.

So, if stories that reflect the hero's journey of the mythic structure resonate with people, and our hearts yearn for the themes they portray, could it be that these yearnings are God given? Might they be pointing us to a story He wants us to encounter? Perhaps the stories we wish were true are those that reflect the story that **is** true.

As we will discover in the next chapter, fantasy literature has always carried readers into other worlds. From Middle-earth to Narnia, from

Hogwarts School of Witchcraft to a Forks school with vampires—those worlds have the power to awaken within our spirits deep desires that remind us we are made for much, much more.

CHAPTER TWO

THE TRUTH OF MYTH

I took mythology a lot more seriously since I'd become a vampire.[1] —Bella Swan

Before diving into specific themes that emerge in the Twilight Phenomenon, we need to understand a few things about the genre of fantasy literature. The best teacher is a writer who, perhaps more than any other, understood the truth of fantasy—an Oxford professor named C.S. Lewis. Lewis came into Christianity having already immersed himself in the rich world of classic literature, myths, legends, and fables—so he had unique insight into and personal experience with the power of fantasy to influence how we feel, think, and believe. That's why he described the "myth" of Christianity as the foundation to understanding ultimate reality.

> *The heart of Christianity is a myth which is also a fact.... It happens—at a particular date, in a particular place, followed by definable historical consequences.... By becoming fact it does not cease to be myth: that is the miracle.*[2]

Our generation typically uses the word "myth" to describe a story that is not true. Lewis used the word in the classic sense—meaning a story that reflects universal truth. In this context, Christianity is the supreme myth—the true, transcendent story that all others are trying to tell. According to Lewis, we should not be surprised when other cultures, legends, and myths reflect our Hero's journey. We should be surprised when they don't. If ours is the true myth—it seems likely that a yearning within all would point them to a story that is also history. Perhaps the pattern of the Gospel resides within the human heart—pushing its way out in the stories we tell.

Lewis wasn't alone in his view that the stories we love reflect the true story of the Gospel. His colleague and close friend, J.R.R. Tolkien, created what became the most popular fantasy series of the 20th century—*The Lord of the Rings*. The world he created, Middle-earth, is one in which hobbits, elves, dwarfs, and men battle side by side to overcome an evil that threatens to destroy their way of life. It also reflects a greater reality, a true hero's journey revealed in Tolkien's Christian faith. In an essay entitled "On Fairy Stories" he identified the Gospel narrative of Christ's life, death, and resurrection as the ultimate fairy story.

> *The Gospels contain a fairy-story, or a story of a larger kind which embraces all the essence of fairy-stories. They contain many marvels—particularly artistic, beautiful, and moving: "mythical" in their perfect, self-contained significance .... But this story has entered History and the primary world .... This story is supreme; and it is true. Art has been verified. God is the Lord, of angels, and of men—and of elves.[3]*

Another contemporary of Lewis, playwright Dorothy Sayers, put it like this:

> *For Jesus Christ is unique—unique among gods and men. There have been incarnate*

gods a-plenty, and slain-and-resurrected gods not a few; but He is the only God who has a date in history.[4]

Lewis, Tolkien, Sayers, and others recognized, like Joseph Campbell, the pattern residing within the great myths and folklore of all cultures. Unlike Campbell, however, they did not see this pattern undermining the Christian Gospel. Rather, it affirms the truth of the Christian Gospel. A truth based upon something much more profound than mere human experience. A truth based upon the greatest story ever told, written by God Himself.

FANTASY AS TRUTH ENCOUNTER

Most of us know C.S. Lewis as the author of the seven *Chronicles of Narnia* stories. His day job, however, was teaching medieval literature at Oxford and Cambridge Universities. He also wrote some of the most influential defenses of Christianity in the 20th century. Surprisingly, however, the man behind Narnia could just as easily have become a leading antagonist against Christianity. After all, he went to Oxford as a skeptic who considered the Gospel just another myth bringing comfort to the weak minded—offering little to the more sophisticated intellect.

"I believe in no religion," 17-year-old Jack wrote a friend. "There is absolutely no proof for any of them, and from a philosophical standpoint, Christianity is not even the best."[5] By the time he was thirty-two, however, he had a very different view, as expressed in a note to that same friend. "Christianity is God expressing Himself through what we call 'real things,'...namely the actual incarnation, crucifixion, and resurrection."[6]

What made the change? In a word, fantasy. It is no stretch to say that Lewis' faith journey began as a result of reading stories that were dripping with Christian truth—awakening within him a desire for something he didn't possess. Like the wonderful aroma of home-baked cookies invading his nostrils, these stories gave Jack a whiff of joy—making him hungry for the full reality of its source.

In later life, Lewis would credit the author of those stories, 19th-century minister George MacDonald, with having influenced virtually every word he ever wrote—including the *Narnia* tales. At first, Lewis didn't recognize MacDonald's stories or the desire they stirred to be anything Christian. Only later, after having found the aroma's source, did Lewis realize what had occurred. Lewis said that through MacDonald's fantasy stories he had "crossed a great frontier" that placed him on a quest for joy, a pursuit that would eventually find its source in the same God of Christianity he had abandoned in childhood. And so, thanks to the imagination of George MacDonald, C.S. Lewis found his way home—and was met by a plate of warm cookies.

I had a similar experience sitting in a London recording studio in 1997 while overseeing the Focus on the Family Radio Theatre adaptation of *The Chronicles of Narnia*. With my eyes closed, I listened to voices from behind the glass as the theater of my mind entered into the drama. Each encounter with the great lion Aslan brought a shiver down my spine and a lump to my throat. It was like encountering something—no, some*one* more frightening, yet comforting than any I had ever met before. I found myself moved in ways decades of church attendance and religious instruction had never accomplished. I was catching a whiff of something much more joyous than I knew.

Months later, my 9-year-old son got his own shivers. Our entire family was driving in the car listening to the final production of *The Lion, the Witch and the Wardrobe*. Not a word was spoken as we endured the dreadful scene of Aslan's death on the stone table. A deep sadness rested upon Shaun as he absorbed the injustice and loss. But then,

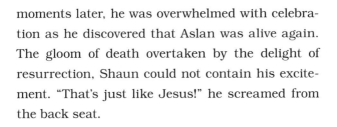

moments later, he was overwhelmed with celebration as he discovered that Aslan was alive again. The gloom of death overtaken by the delight of resurrection, Shaun could not contain his excitement. "That's just like Jesus!" he screamed from the back seat.

Like most kids raised in Sunday school, Shaun had heard the story of Jesus' death and resurrection literally dozens of times. It had become routine, expected, perhaps even boring. But through a fantasy tale that had none of what Lewis called "stained glass and Sunday school associations," Shaun was caught off guard—surprised by the most wonderful and potent truth of Christian faith. The effect on his heart, like my own sitting in that studio, was a whiff of true delight. We entered into the experience of the Gospel rather than merely exploring its tenets. And along the way, we "crossed a great frontier" that awakened a new, more vibrant faith.

What George MacDonald did for the faith and imagination of C.S. Lewis, Lewis has done for millions who enjoy his fantasy tales. With combined sales of over 65 million copies, and the inspiration behind the recent feature film, the seven *Chronicles of Narnia* books are more popular than ever. And with good reason. With the possible exception of J.R.R. Tolkien, no 20th-century writer more masterfully married the enchantment of fantasy with the enrichment of faith. The Narnia stories are like a meal with the nourishment of meat and vegetables, but the taste of cake and candy. Both the dreams of fairyland and the promise of Heaven invade the imagination at the same time, baptizing it with wonderful and unexpected effects.

The problem, of course, is that we rarely associate pleasure with nourishment. The Narnia tales are such good children's stories, we resist the notion that they allegorize the Gospel story. Lewis himself debunked the notion that his tales are mere Christian allegory, explaining that the Christian truths pushed their way into the story on their own. His theology was part of him, so became part of what he created—like air bubbling to the water's surface.

Some people seem to think that I began by asking myself how I could say something about Christianity to children; then fixed on the fairy tale as an instrument; then collected information about child-psychology and decided what age group I'd write for; then drew up a list of basic Christian truths and hammered out "allegories" to

*embody them. This is all pure moonshine.
I couldn't write in that way at all. Everything began with images; a faun carrying an umbrella, a queen on a sledge, a
magnificent lion. At first there wasn't anything Christian about them; that element
pushed itself in of its own accord. It was
part of the bubbling.[7]*

The Narnia stories are not allegory. They rather grow out of a central supposition. Suppose there existed another world peopled by animals rather than human beings. Suppose that world fell, like ours, and had in it someone the equivalent of Christ.

Aslan entered Narnia in the form of a lion just as Jesus came into this world in the form of a man. Based upon this supposition, Lewis created a fantasy world that depicts the central theme of our real world—redemption through the incarnate God's death and resurrection. The magical part is that this mythical Christ somehow draws us ever deeper to the real.

In May 1955, the mother of a 9-year-old boy named Laurence wrote to C.S. Lewis explaining that Laurence was concerned that he loved Aslan more than Jesus. To her delighted surprise, she received a reply ten days later that included the following:

> *Laurence can't really love Aslan more than Jesus, even if he feels that's what he is doing. For the things he loves Aslan for doing or saying are simply the things Jesus really did and said. So that when Laurence thinks he is loving Aslan, he is really loving Jesus: and perhaps loving Him more than he ever did before.*[8]

According to Lewis himself, part of what makes the adventure into the wardrobe so exciting is the worldview that lies behind the wardrobe.

WORLDVIEW

We all have a worldview whether we know it or not. Perhaps we've heard the word thrown around by a teacher, minister, or while reading an article or book. But what, exactly, is a "worldview" and why should we care while reading a series like *Twilight?* Have you ever visited an optometrist to have your eyes examined? You may have been asked to place your face against a machine to read the letters on a chart. I have such poor eyesight that I could only read a few lines before letters turned fuzzy and obscure. And then, almost like magic, the doctor flipped a few lenses in front of my eyes to give me a better view. I'll never forget the day I got glasses and discovered details and richness around me I had previously missed. I am reminded of the contrast each time I remove my glasses. My sight shifts from crystal clear to rather blurry in an instant.

Put simply, a worldview can be defined as the lenses through which we view the world. These lenses are significantly shaped by our spiritual and religious perspective. Which lenses we wear will heavily influence what we perceive from the books we read and movies viewed. A skeptical atheist, for example, might read the *Twilight* series and see nothing more than fuzzy superstition. They might enjoy the story as fantasy, but not as a "myth" reflecting truth. A perceptive Christian, on the other hand, can see the detail and rich color in themes like good and evil or romantic love because both grow out of profoundly spiritual realities. Again, it depends upon which lenses one wears while reading.

Do you remember the story of Saint Paul's visit to Athens, Greece? Athens was the artistic and intellectual capital of Paul's day and ancient home to such philosophical giants as Plato and Aristotle. Athens also served as the world's religious capital, birthplace to a mythological convergence that had come to dominate the Roman Empire.

While on layover to Corinth, Paul entered into dialogue with the city's academic elite—those who no doubt prided themselves on cutting-edge thinking and open-minded acceptance. Surrounded by altars celebrating gods from every perspective under the Roman sun, evidence of their religious tolerance literally stared Paul in the face as he presented his own brand of belief. Much like Socrates had done centuries earlier, Paul entered one first-century Starbucks after another to engage in philosophical discourse. Before long, word spread that some Jewish guy from a remote corner of the empire was pushing a new, foreign religion.

"Come and tell us more about this new religion," they said. "You are saying some rather startling things, and we want to know what it's all about."

Keep in mind, discussing the latest ideas is what people in Athens did. Missing the opening of a new philosophy would be as unthinkable as New York critics missing the latest Broadway play. So a crowd quickly gathered to hear Paul make his case.

"Men of Athens, I notice that you are very religious..." Paul must have winked as the audience chuckled at such an understatement, "...for as I was walking along I saw your many altars."

These "many altars" visibly expressed a view commonly accepted in this time that every religious myth was equally valid because none were necessarily true in an ultimate sense. Few in the pagan world actually believed their idol to be a deity, especially among the educated class. They saw them as symbols, icons of a greater reality. No one knew which (if any) mythology most accurately reflected the real story of God. They covered their bases, if you will, bringing all religious stories together in one place, hoping their collective script might express a more transcendent tale. But instead of connecting them to the authentically supernatural, they created a culture superstitious in the extreme.

Paul continues, "And one of these altars had this inscription on it—'To an Unknown God.' You have been worshiping Him without knowing who He is, and now I wish to tell you about Him."

At this point you might have heard a collective gasp of surprise and intrigue—surprise because few dared claim certain knowledge of the true God, yet intrigued by Paul's piercing insight into their deeper motives.

Why establish an altar "To an Unknown God"? I can think of two reasons. First, weary of trying to keep up with the latest religious fad, exasperated city council members may have wanted to stop the costly proliferation of new construction projects. Enough blasted idols already! But likely a far more substantial reason prompted them to create the unnamed idol. Recognizing their own imperfect knowledge, an altar to the unknown God might better express what all the others tried to say. Like their hero, Socrates, the Athenians sensed there had to be a real God out there somewhere, even if His particular name and description remained a mystery. When Paul claimed knowledge of this God, ears perked up.

"He is the God who made the world and everything in it. Since He is Lord of Heaven and earth, He doesn't live in man-made temples...He Himself gives life and breath to everything, and He satisfies every need there is."

After describing the God of all power, Paul made an amazing statement.

"His purpose in all of this was that the nations should seek after God and *perhaps feel their way toward Him and find Him—though He is not far from any of us.*" Deep within every man and woman throbs both the desire and capacity to "feel their way toward" the God who, in Paul's words, "is not far from any of us." Yes, there exists a real God our idols only suggest. He wants to be known. He can be known. Everything we are grows out of the fact that we are His offspring. Paul explains further that God can overlook people's former ignorance, inviting them out of mythic shadows into the light of a true story. A story all others are trying to tell. A story that is a myth turned fact by invading history.

THREE QUESTIONS

Paul's conversation on Mar's Hill reminds us that stories are the imagination's way of reaching for the "true myth" ultimately revealed in the Gospel of Jesus Christ. How? By touching upon three questions every worldview must answer.

Question #1: What are we made for?

Regardless of religious perspective, every one of us senses that life has to be more than meets the eye. We find contentment difficult to achieve because we know we were made for more. The mundane routine of the daily grind doesn't satisfy that deep, persistent longing within. And it never will.

We create wonders that point to the wonder that created us. We tell stories that suggest a transcendent author. We feel emotions that reflect God's tender heart. But most of all, we yearn for something that seems out of reach.

C.S. Lewis put it like this: "If I find in myself a desire that no experience in this world can satisfy, the most probable explanation is that I was made for another world."[9]

Deep down, we know we were made for more.

Question #2: What is wrong with our world?

After months of joyous anticipation, little Matthew is born. But something is wrong. He enters the world deaf and mostly blind. Years later, he displays signs of what turns out to be a rare nervous disorder. So begins the difficult life of our now 28-year-old nephew.

A relative newlywed and father of 1-year-old Bradley, Don boarded a Phoenix-bound plane a few days before reuniting with his wife and child. He had to get back to the office. Lori and Bradley stayed behind for a second week with family in Detroit. Minutes later, news images flashed across the television screen announcing the crash. A call awoke me that night, informing me that my boyhood pal and best man had died in the flames, along with nearly 200 others.

A small story buried deep within the mid-week paper describes how a 4-year-old boy found his father's gun. Lovingly playing with his 18-month old baby sister, he points the "toy" at her and pulls the trigger. The bullet explodes her laughing face. Police say that when they arrived, the weeping boy cried out to his dazed mommy: "It was an accident! I didn't mean to do it!"

Such moments reveal a world that seems cruel and heartless. One need not celebrate many birthdays to know that we live in a broken world. Philosophers call it the problem of evil. For many, it is the primary obstacle to belief in God. We want good but see bad. Best-selling book titles reflect our attempts to reconcile the seeming contradiction.

When Bad Things Happen to Good People

When God Doesn't Make Sense

Where is God When It Hurts?

"With so much pain in the world," we wonder, "how can anyone believe in a good God?" Simplistic answers do not work. Philosophical explanations do not satisfy. Compassionate sympathy feels nice, but fails to remove the heartache. Life hurts, and we want it to stop!

Sickness. Suffering. Tyranny. Tragedy. Crime. Cruelty. Depression. Death. They all point to the second reality we all know. Something is wrong.

Question #3: How will it be made right?

Like the tension of an unresolved musical chord, the wrong of life creates a yearning for resolution within the human heart. Yes, something is wrong. But leaving it there would drive us mad. We must move on to tenet three. We want it to be made right.

Every "once upon a time" requires a "happily ever after," or we leave the story feeling cheated. Every mother's son killed in battle begs for a nation's gratitude to soothe the pain of loss. Every villain seeking destruction demands a hero seeking justice. Every descent into the darkness of depression pleads in silence for a return to the light of joy.

Even while shaking our fist in anger at a God who seems cruel or distant, we reach for a God we hope can set things right and redeem our pain for a greater good. We don't know how. We don't know when. But we know things should not, cannot be left wrong. They must be made right again.

Stay tuned and you'll discover how, if read through Christian lenses, even vampire love stories reflect our inescapable desire to find answers to all three worldview questions.

CHAPTER THREE

THE REALITY OF VAMPIRES

*Of course, their legends say the same of us.
That we must be destroyed. That we are
soulless murderers.*[1] —Edward Cullen

Will the sun burn you up if you go outside during the day?

Have you ever changed into a bat?

What's it like to sleep in a coffin?

Have you ever met Frankenstein's monster?

What questions would you ask someone who claimed to be a vampire? Early in their relationship Bella pieces together clues that cause her to realize the truth about the Cullen clan. So she asks Edward a series of questions to sort out truth from fiction when it comes to vampires.

> *"Don't laugh—but how can you come out during the daytime?"*
>
> *He laughed anyway. "Myth."*
>
> *"Burned by the sun?"*
>
> *"Myth."*
>
> *"Sleeping in coffins?"*
>
> *"Myth."*[2]

I've never asked such questions, possibly because I've never met an actual vampire. At least, I didn't think I had before learning the meaning of vampirism. Now I'm not so sure.

To properly explore the Twilight Phenomenon, we need to discover what makes vampires and other monsters so fascinating. Believe it or not, there is a long history and unsettling reality behind the fictional characters that appear on the pages of books and in the scenes of movies.

First, let me clarify that I do not believe in the literal existence of human-like creatures with sharp fangs that turn into bats. Count Dracula is a fictional character, not a historical person. What he represents, however, is very real—and very disturbing. As we will discover, the truth behind vampirism is much more frightening than the fiction of vampires.

Have you ever asked yourself why we seem so drawn to evil characters in our stories? We love to hate the wicked witch, the cruel tyrant, the evil villain, and the hideous creature. We pay good money to sit in a dark theater in order to be frightened half to death by creaking doors, dark corridors, and dreadful monsters. Then we wake up in the middle of the night panicked over what we tell ourselves was "just a nightmare." But deep down we know that the scary images of human imagination point to something truly frightening in our world.

Do you remember the second question every worldview must answer: "What is wrong with our world?" The scary stories we tell suggest a disturbing answer rooted in very dark realities.

WHAT IS VAMPIRISM?

When most of us use the word *vampire* we refer to fictional characters found in stories. We don't believe they really exist. Yet all of us fear what they represent, *vampirism*. A full picture of vampirism comes from reading several definitions.

Believe it or not, there are actual people who call themselves vampires in our world. Curious about how they describe themselves, I discovered the word can be applied to certain dysfunctional behaviors. Michelle Belanger, editor of an anthology titled *Vampires in Their Own Words*, described a vampiric identity known as psychic vampires, individuals who are "driven to feed upon the energy of others." She explains that many psychic vampires are unaware of their condition which causes others to develop "methods of protecting one's energy from individuals perceived as psychic predators" who are "needy and clingy emotional parasites."[3]

Another definition comes from the most recent edition of the Random House Dictionary which describes vampirism as "unscrupulous exploitation, ruin, or degradation of others."[4] Let's unpack each of those words:

- Unscrupulous: They have no regard for moral rules or restrictions.

- Exploitation: They take advantage of the unfortunate.

- Ruin: They tear down what is strong and corrupt what is good.

- Degradation: They disfigure the beautiful and spoil the sacred.

Notice that this definition specifies doing these things to "others." Many people get involved in unscrupulous activities that exploit, ruin, or degrade themselves. But vampirism means extending that destruction to those around us—including those closest to us.

A third helpful definition comes from the highly respected Merriam-Webster's Medical Dictionary which calls vampirism "a sexual perversion in which pleasure and especially sexual pleasure is obtained by the drawing of the blood."[5] Don't be surprised. It is no accident that so many vampire stories, including the *Twilight* series, inter-mingle intense erotic attraction with the thirst for blood. We will explore the reasons for that later. For now, however, it is enough to know there is a direct connection between the two.

In short, vampirism is the process of draining life from others—from the joy-robbing annoyance of "please don't leave me" neediness to the ruinous abuse of rape. These and other "blood sucking" influences deplete that which gives us a vital life and undermines that which gives us human dignity.

WHY VAMPIRES?

So what prompted the fictional embodiment of vampirism called vampires? It is impossible to pinpoint a precise point in time or event that spawned the first vampire myth. But we can scan the horizon of history to discover vampire superstitions that have emerged in a variety of cultures.[6]

- German folklore told of shape-shifting spirits associated with nightmares called "Alps." These beings appeared as butterfly, cat, birds, and dog-like vampires emerging from the breath of a demon. They were said to suck the life breath of their victims. Alps were also said to cause disturbing dreams as they sexually molested or drank the blood of victims.[7]

- A vampire "cult" emerged in Eastern Europe so widespread that a respected scholar named Dom

Augustine Calmet began collecting information compiled and published as a two-volume work in 1746. He rejected the notion of vampires on intellectual grounds and because he could not reconcile claims with the teachings of Christianity. But he did report on strange occurrences in Hungary, Moravia, and Silesia.[8]

- Japanese lore described an ogre demon boy that wore red and gorged himself on blood of women before being defeated by the medieval hero named Raiko who decapitates the ogre and frees the female captives.[9]

- In Malaysian lore, women who died during childbirth became demons that consumed the blood of newborns, nursing mothers, and pregnant women. Often appearing in the form of an owl, they drank their victim's blood from a hole in the base of the neck.[10]

- Russian folklore associated those who reject the truth (heretics) with vampires. In fact, the *eretic* was an ordinary person who had his or her body invaded by an evil sorcerer (heretic). This vampire would first stalk and devour the victim's family before moving on to others. In another variation, *erecticy* were women who sold their souls to the devil while alive and came back after death as vampires to seduce people away from Christianity.[11]

- European Gypsies considered vampires the ultimate occult evil and held various beliefs about how they came into being. Some thought a person who lived a sinful life (such as bandits) turned into vampires at death. Others thought men who harmed others or failed to ask forgiveness for their sins rose as a ghost and then took on a human form outside the grave. Those who had many lovers in life were thought to become the most dangerous vampires after death.

> A married vampire was believed to
> visit his wife on the seventh night
> after burial to have sex. If single,
> he would seek out young women,
> divorcees, or widows.[12]

Throughout history men and women have invented stories that mix hard fact with hard-to-swallow fiction when they encounter something real that can't be explained. Vampire cults and myths seem to have arisen as superstitious responses to unseen realities. Some "unseen realities" are spiritual mysteries. Others are unseen because they are too small for the naked eye. Imagine living in a world that knew nothing about germs, the immune system, or contagious diseases. It is easy for us to dismiss such tendencies today because we understand medical science. But when medieval peasants saw an otherwise healthy man rapidly deteriorate and die, they might have tried imagining "unseen" forces at work—especially after his burial when the man's wife starts looking pale and lifeless, followed by his children, and neighbors. Imagine the fear they felt as the mysterious spirit of death spread throughout their tiny village.

Many believe that vampire stories grew out of such scenarios. "Typically, the vampire of European folklore targets friends and family members for his or her nightly predations," explains Belanger "leading scholars to suggest that vampirism was merely a convenient myth that grew up to explain instances of contagion, when a wasting sickness made its way through an entire extended family or village."[13]

Whatever the reasons, we know that vampire legends and myths have been around for a long time in a variety of cultures. The most common characteristics of these mythic creatures tell us that they are:

- **Blood Drinkers**: Everyone knows that vampires drink blood. Some consume human blood, others animal blood. They take blood to sustain their own existence by robbing the living of life. According to Eastern European folklore beliefs, blood has great magical potency.[14]

- **Shape-Shifters**: To change oneself from one form to another is called *metamorphosis* or *shape-shifting*. We typically think of Dracula becoming a bat, but vampires have also been said to transform into cats, snakes, birds, wolves, and even horses. The idea of shape-shifting may have grown out of Norse mythology where gods and demons were known to take on human or animal forms.[15]

- **Cross Haters**: In Bram Stocker's classic novel, the vampire's nemesis is Professor Abraham Van Helsing. Many find it surprising that Van Helsing is a very religious character who seems more Christian priest than monster hunter. He considers vampires an emissary of satan on earth. In fact, one of Van Helsing's most potent weapons against Dracula is the cross. Why? Because as creatures that embody all that is unholy, vampires despise all things sacred.

- **Garlic Avoiders**: Garlic is a type of onion that commonly emerges in vampire lore. In Romania, for example, those who refuse to eat garlic were identified as living vampires. In other parts of Europe they might toast someone with the phrase "here's garlic in your eyes" because garlic was said to ward off evil eye. And in China they protected children from vampires by wetting the child's forehead with garlic. In the Philippines they rubbed garlic onto armpits. Garlic has also been stuffed in the mouths of corpses and thrown onto coffins and gravesites to keep vampires from leaving the grave.[16]

- **Lust Indulgers**: Show me a vampire and I'll show you a lust-driven creature. The two are inseparably linked. Throughout vampire lore and literature, vampires are compulsively driven to satisfy wicked urges. Many modern vampire tales read more like a pornographic romance novel than gothic horror. Vampiric blood-thirst reflects more than hunger pains or the need for nourishment. It suggests an insatiable craving for sexual gratification.

- **Undead Creatures**: Commonly described as the "undead," vampires endure an existence somewhere between life and death. Like demons, angels who were banished from their proper place, vampires exist in exile haunted by the memory of human joys now out of reach. Once a mysterious union of flesh and spirit, they have become a twisted mix of human and demonic. Unlike both, however, they are now cut off from either the hope of Heaven or the damnation of hell. Vampires wander the eternal limbo of displacement. Louis, the main vampire in Anne Rice's *Interview with the Vampire,* hates his immortal existence with no hope of any resolution. "What consolation it would be to know Satan," he admits, "to look upon his face, no matter how terrible that countenance was, to know that I belonged to him totally, and thus put to rest forever the torment of this ignorance. To step through some veil that would forever separate me from all that I called human nature."[17] These "undead" creatures would prefer hell to the existence they endure.

Vampire Hall of Fame

Stephenie Meyer's *Twilight* books will likely be added to the vampire hall of fame, if such a place exists, due to their immense popularity. Her installment will follow a long line of fictional novels and screenplays that have made vampire tales such a popular genre over the centuries. Some of the most well-known and influential include:

- ***The Vampyre***: You've probably never heard of it, but the 1819 short story by John William Polidori called *The Vampyre* is considered by many to be the spark that lit the flame of the romantic vampire genre in fantasy literature. His story has been described as "the first to fuse the disparate elements of vampirism into a coherent literary genre." Polidori's story "exploited the gothic horror predilections of the public" and "transformed the vampire from a character in folklore into the form that is recognized today—an aristocratic fiend who preys among high society."[18] The inspiration for Polidori's tale came during an unusually rainy summer when he and several friends passed the time by sharing ghost stories. Polidori crafted his short tale over "two or three idle mornings." Mary Shelley, a mere teen who was also part of the house-bound group, went on to create one of the most famous gothic horror books of all time, *Frankenstein*.[19]

- **Dracula**: Without question the most famous of all vampire tales, Bram Stoker's *Dracula* was published in 1897. Up until a few weeks before publication Stoker titled the book *The Undead*. He also had a different name for the vampire until becoming intrigued by the Romanian word *dracul* which means "devil." In the novel, Count Dracula is a shape-shifting, blood-drinking, undead being who leaves his Transylvanian castle to terrorize victims in London—most notably a newly wed bride named Lucy whom he ravishes and turns into a vampire. There have been many film adaptations of Dracula, starting with the 1931 version staring Bela Lugosi as the black-cape wearing Count. The character of Count Dracula has appeared in 130 of the near 700 vampire films ever made.[20] The story has also been adapted many times for the stage, including a musical version that appeared on Broadway in 2004. The novel was written as a series of letters, journal entries, and legal documents that layer upon one another to reveal the chilling tale. Those who have never read it may be surprised to learn that the original book reads, at times, like a religious document. The vampire is described as a servant of darkness while those who dismiss unseen realities are criticized. "It is the fault of our science that it wants to explain all; and if it explain not, then it says there is nothing to explain."[21]   Dracula's nemesis is a deeply religious man named Van Helsing who says that the devil "may work against us for all he's worth, but God sends us men when we want them."[22] Describing Dracula as a "man-eater" who prowls unceasingly with a thirst for human blood, Van Helsing says the vampire has come from the devil so they must risk "even our own souls for the safety of one we love—for the good of mankind, and for the honour and glory of God."[23] Dracula is described as a selfish being confining himself to one remorseless purpose. "We, however, are not selfish, and we believe that God is with us through all this blackness, and these many dark hours."[24] The message of the book is clear. A devil like Dracula can only be defeated by virtuous men willing to sacrifice themselves for others and to serve a holy God.

- ***I Am Legend***: A 1954 novel by Richard Matheson called *I Am Legend* later became a 2007 blockbuster film starring Will Smith, although the film version deviates quite a bit from the original story. (Earlier film adaptations include *The Last Man on Earth* in 1964 and *The Omega Man* in 1971.) The hero, Robert Neville, is the last survivor of a bacterial plague that has killed most and turned everyone else into vampires. Neville spends his days hunting vampires and heads into his fortressed home after dark. Matheson's novel was the first to portray vampires as victims of a contagious disease rather than monsters who choose evil. In the end, Neville realizes that he has become the "legend"—one a now changed humanity views as the threatening villain. The book hints at an evolutionary process that makes humans into something else and redefines "normal."[25]

- ***Interview with a Vampire***: One of the most successful vampire novelists of all time is Anne Rice, author of the 1976 book introducing the world to the menacing vampire named Lestat and his victim turned fellow-vampire Louis. Both characters made it to the big screen, portrayed by actors Tom Cruise and Brad Pitt in the 1994 film version of the book. The story unfolds as a news reporter invites Louis to tell his 200-year history that began on his slave plantation near New Orleans in the late 18th century. That's when Lestat turned Louis into a vampire against his will. Like the "vegetarian" vampires of *Twilight*, Louis initially feeds on the blood of animals due to his reverence for human life. But that changes as he becomes overtaken by the thirst for human blood. Lestat and Louis later become enemies. Louis also encounters wicked old-world vampires while living in Europe whom he must destroy in order to gain his own freedom. Returning to a solitary existence in America, Louis grows weary of his undead existence. The news reporter, on the other hand, becomes attracted to the potential for immortality and power and begs Louis to turn him into a vampire. Louis refuses, so the reporter instead seeks out Lestat. *Interview with the Vampire* launched author Anne Rice, who went on to write a series of similar stories featuring Lestat.[26]

LIVING NIGHTMARES

As scary as the vampires of literature and film may be, none of them strike terror in the heart like the real-life vampirism documented through the ages.

- **The Real Dracula**: The name of Bram Stoker's famous vampire was inspired by a 15th-century prince commonly called *Vlad Dracul* or *Vlad the Impaler*. His favorite form of torture and execution was to impale his enemies on posts where they were left to a sometimes slow and tortured death. While the numbers may be exaggerated, Vlad is credited with impaling about 80,000 victims. German stories describe impaling, torturing, burning, skinning, roasting, cutting off limbs, boiling people, and feeding their flesh to friends or relatives. His cruelty extended to people of every age, including children and babies. One account of his atrocities said that, "He caused so much pain and suffering that even the most bloodthirstiest persecutors of Christianity like Herodes, Nero, Diocletian, and all other pagans combined hadn't even thought of." Vlad's method of torture included gradually forcing the body onto a sharpened stake which he usually had oiled. He didn't want the stake too sharp because he didn't want the victim to die from sudden shock. As a result, death by impalement was slow and painful with some victims suffering for hours or days, and the dead corpses were often left to decay for months. One claim says that in the year 1460, 10,000 people were impaled on a single day near Vlad's home in Transylvania. A different accuses Vlad of impaling 30,000 merchants and officials from another Transylvanian city for defying his authority. Vlad's Romanian surname (Draculea) means Son of Dracula, derived from his father's title "Vlad the devil." (In Romanian the word Dracula means "devil" or "dragon.") Vlad the Impaler is referenced as "Dracula" in several documents from his time.[27]

- **Blood Bath**: A 16th-century Transylvanian noblewoman earned the nickname "Blood Countess" due to her sadistic treatment of pretty servant and peasant girls. Elizabeth Bathory held the bizarre belief that she could retain her youthful beauty if she bathed in a virgin's blood. So that's what she did. Over the years she lured hundreds of girls into her service before torturing and then bleeding them for her beauty treatment regiment. Some of her cruelties included taking "blood showers" by sitting beneath caged victims alternatively poked with sharp spikes and burning irons. She was also known to pour cold water on naked girls standing in freezing snow and force them to eat the cooked flesh of other servants. This all took place in an era when nobles had little concern for the poor peasant population. In fact, Bathory's evil ways may have gone unnoticed had she not begun victimizing daughters of nobility. When these girls disappeared, rumors spread. Her wicked history became public knowledge after several noblemen, priests, and others inspected her castle. They found the remains of about 50 mutilated bodies along with several living victims caged like animals. It is said that Bathory's own journal records the names of more than 600 victims.[28]

- **The Vampire Butcher**: In the early 20th century a German butcher named Fritz Haarman molested and murdered at least 24 homeless boys. Known as the "Vampire Butcher of Hanover," Haarman killed the boys by biting into their jugular vein and drinking their blood. His victims fell between the ages of 12 and 18. Many of their bodies were believed to have been ground into sausage, cooked, and eaten.[29]

- **Acid Bath Vampire:** A bit closer to our own generation, a 20th-century Englishman named John George Haigh earned the nickname "Acid Bath Vampire" after a series of nine murders during the 1940s. Haigh dissolved his victim's bodies in sulphuric acid before selling their possessions to collect substantial sums of money. He mistakenly assumed police needed a body before they could bring a charge of murder.[30] While I found no official reports suggesting blood-lust,

Haigh's crimes did inspire a bizarre heavy metal song by the group Macabre titled *Acid Bath Vampire* that includes chilling lyrics like "You will die by surprise. When I take your life, I will smile. John George Haigh was a vampire who drank old ladies' blood then put them in a non-corrosive drum and with acid he'd dissolve them. With my knife I make a cut on your neck. Your blood fills a glass for me, a special treat."[31]

Sadly, human history is filled with examples of our capacity for vampiric cruelty to one another. These, and other incidents point to a very dark reality our scariest vampire stories merely shadow.

A Dark Reality

Lurking beneath vampire myths, folklore, novels, and infamous murderers is the reality of a dark enemy. Many of the things we imagine are rooted in things that are; none more so than tales of seductive, life-stealing villains. Consider some of the characteristics attributed to satan in the Scriptures.

- **Shape-Shifter:** The devil is described as one who takes on different forms such as a serpent, a dragon, an angel of light, and a lion. His demons are also said to inhabit human and animal bodies.

He laid hold of the dragon, that serpent of old, who is the Devil and Satan... (Revelation 20:2).

Satan himself transforms himself into an angel of light (2 Corinthians 11:14).

Your adversary the devil walks about like a roaring lion, seeking whom he may devour (1 Peter 5:8).

And when He had come out of the boat, immediately there met Him out of the tombs a man with an unclean spirit, who had his dwelling among the tombs...night and day, he was in the mountains and in the tombs, crying out and cutting himself with stones...So all the demons begged Him, saying "Send us to the swine, that we may enter them." And at once Jesus gave them permission. Then the unclean spirits went out and entered the swine... (Mark 5:2-13).

• **Murderous Liar:** Satan is cunning and seductive like the vampires inspired by his reality. His most powerful and persistent weapon is the art of deception because those who are deceived don't know it. They are easily led to their own destruction because they willingly follow a map filled with lies. What some call "spiritual warfare" is no more than a battle between truth and lies.

Now the serpent was more cunning than any beast of the field which the Lord God had made... Then the serpent said to the woman, "You will not surely die" (Genesis 3:1-4).

"You are of your father the devil, and the desires of your father you want to do. He was a murderer from the beginning, and does not stand in the truth, because there is no truth in him. When he speaks a lie, he speaks from his own resources, for he is a liar and the father of it. But because

I tell the truth, you do not believe Me" (Jesus in John 8:44-45).

- **Cross Hater:** The devil cowers before the cross because it represents his greatest defeat. Of course, there was a time when satan loved the cross. He relished in victory as soldiers nailed Jesus' hands into the harsh wood. He celebrated in glee when they raised the cross upward so that our Lord would struggle to breathe under the weight of his own body. The devil and his demons thought they had won the war when those who once shouted "Hosanna!" instead screamed "Crucify Him!" as blood drained from Jesus' head and body. Imagine the look on lucifer's face when, just a few days later, he realized the cross was actually a tool in God's hands to rescue humanity from satan's life-stealing power!

"O Death, where is your sting? O Hades, where is your victory?"...But thanks be to God, who gives us the victory through

our Lord Jesus Christ (1 Corinthians 15:55,57).

He humbled Himself and became obedient to the point of death, even the death of the cross. Therefore God also has highly exalted Him and given Him the name which is above every name (Philippians 2:8-9).

And having disarmed the powers and authorities, he made a public spectacle of them, triumphing over them by the **cross** (Colossians 2:15 NIV, emphasis mine).

All evil, including satan's vampirism, is rooted in madness. What kind of madness? The kind that deludes and disconnects itself from the ultimate reality that there is one God and we aren't Him. Just as vampires were human beings with tremendous potential for joy and life, satan was made for much more than he became. In fact, he was once the highest-ranking archangel. Before his rebellion, lucifer was bright, articulate, and adorned with splendid beauty. He had it all. In a passage most scholars agree is describing lucifer, Ezekiel gives us a snapshot of what he was like while serving God.

THE TWILIGHT PHENOMENON

> *You were the model of perfection, full
> of wisdom and perfect in beauty. You
> were in Eden, the garden of God; every
> precious stone adorned you: ruby, topaz
> and emerald, chrysolite, onyx and jasper,
> sapphire, turquoise and beryl. Your
> settings and mountings were made of
> gold; on the day you were created they
> were prepared* (Ezekiel 28:12-13 NIV).

Ezekiel also describes the position he held in
God's domain.

> *You were anointed as a guardian cherub,
> for so I ordained you. You were on the
> holy mount of God; you walked among
> the fiery stones* (Ezekiel 28:14 NIV).

Lucifer was ordained by God to serve in his
inner circle as "guardian cherub" over "Eden, the
garden of God." The precise meaning is uncer-
tain. But it seems to represent an honored post
only worthy of the most trusted servant. We know
Eden as the place God would perform and place
his greatest work of creation. It is doubtful any
domain was as near and dear to God's heart. So,
like any wise ruler, He placed it under the pro-
tection and jurisdiction of His most talented and

gifted steward—lucifer. And for a time he executed that responsibility flawlessly.

> *You were blameless in your ways from the day you were created...* (Ezekiel 28:15 NIV).

But one day, for some reason, everything changed.

> *You were blameless in your ways from the day you were created till wickedness was found in you. Through your widespread trade you were filled with violence, and you sinned....Your heart became proud on account of your beauty, and you corrupted your wisdom because of your splendor...* (Ezekiel 28:15-17 NIV).

Dig below the surface of all evil and you will find the root—pride. It is pride that demands its way, refuses to submit, rebels against authority, and inflates its own sense of worth beyond sanity. And it is pride that drives the created one to shake his fist in the face of his Creator and demand the throne.

> *You said in your heart, "I will ascend*
> *to heaven; I will raise my throne above*
> *the stars of God; I will sit enthroned on*
> *the mount of assembly, on the utmost*
> *heights of the sacred mountain. I will*
> *ascend above the tops of the clouds; I*
> *will make myself like the Most High"*
> (Isaiah 14:13-14 NIV).

This is the insanity of pride. One who was spoken into existence by God saw himself as God's equal. Unwilling to remain an honored servant, lucifer made his play for the top role; a delusional boycott of reality, mad as a mouse declaring himself to be a lion, foolish as a tree cutting itself off from its life-sustaining roots.

Death is the opposite of life. It is not the end of existence, but the beginning of something far worse; an eternity of madness, separated from the source of sanity; continual deception, denying the clarity of truth. Demanding the freedom to control his own destiny, lucifer became a slave to his own hatred. Jesus said that he who wishes to find his life must lose it. Lucifer got it backward. As a result, he gave birth to death.

Sadly, humankind followed in lucifer's footsteps when we joined his rebellion. The third chapter of

Genesis describes our first ancestors tainting the blood of our race by accepting satan's lie that "you will be like God, knowing good from evil." He didn't mean we would know *about* evil (mere intellectual recognition) but rather that we would *know* evil (actual experience). We were never meant to experience hatred, pain, despair, and death. But we do. That's because we live on a battlefield where humanity wars against itself.

When all is said and done, we must recognize that the seductive, life-draining, deceptive realities of vampirism are rooted in dark tendencies of the human heart. We were created for goodness, but our fallen nature causes us to rebel against what is good and crave what is bad. Like the book *I Am Legend* imagines, humanity changed due to a contagious disease that spread to all but one. As Jesus, the One, put it "men loved darkness rather than light, because their deeds were evil" (John 3:19). The apostle Paul said it like this, "Therefore, just as through one man sin entered the world, and death through sin, and thus death spread to all men, because all sinned" (Rom. 5:12).

No wonder human history is filled with tales that reflect the continual battle between the joy of life and the horrors of death.

Vampires, while fictional, echo chilling realities of the human condition. First, that we have been deceived by one who seeks to drain away the life God intended us to know. Second, that our race tends to rebel against good—making the seductive allure of evil something we crave rather than resist. And finally, we are haunted by the memory of the kind of life we were made to experience. A haunting, as we will discover, that makes the Twilight Phenomenon much more profound and important than many have recognized.

CHAPTER FOUR

LOVE HUNGER

About three things I was absolutely positive. First, Edward was a vampire. Second, there was a part of him...that thirsted for my blood. And third, I was unconditionally and irrevocably in love with him. —Bella Swan

Once upon a time there was a teenage girl who, while minding her own business, fell madly in love with an irresistibly handsome boy. The boy belonged to a dangerous clan suspected of murder. The girl and boy enjoyed a series of secret rendezvous and became more and more attached to one another. When others learned of the romance they strongly disapproved; the girl's people fearing for her safety, the boy's worried he was playing with fire. But neither could imagine life without the other. So they threw caution to the wind and risked their lives to protect their love.

Recognize the story? If you thought *Twilight*, you are close. If you thought *Romeo and Juliet*, you are much closer.

Anyone who has read or watched Shakespeare's famous love story will see strong parallels in the story of Bella and Edward. Juliet, like Bella, lives in a world where a long-term rivalry exists between her people (the house of Capulet) and Romeo's people (the house of Montague). Like the vampires and werewolves in the *Twilight* series, these two clans have been feuding for some time, to the point of violence and murder. A delicate truce is put into place, but the animosity between the clans continues—creating a serious obstacle for Romeo and Juliet to overcome. Unaware that the two have secretly wed, Juliet's family arranges for her to marry someone else. On the night before the wedding, however, Juliet conspires with a Friar who gives her a drug that will make her appear dead for two days. It worked. The grieving family placed her in the family crypt. According to Juliet's plan, the Friar would inform Romeo and tell him to meet her at the tomb as she wakes so the two can run off together. But word never reaches Romeo, so he thinks Juliet died. In the closing scene, a heart-broken Romeo kills himself. Juliet wakes up to discover her dead lover. She too commits suicide knowing she cannot bear to live without him.

It is a common theme; two people so madly in love that life seems pointless without the other. In the legend of *Tristan and Isolde,* for example, the two enemies fall in love after drinking a love potion. Unable to openly declare that love, they meet in the forest at night under the cover of darkness. During the day they pretend apathy toward one another, but after the sun goes down they reunite in romantic intimacy. Isolde says that only in "the long night of death" can the two be united forever. She gets her wish when Tristan dies after a sword fight, causing Isolde to die from intense grief.

In *West Side Story,* it is a girl named Maria who falls in love with an enemy named Tony. The obstacle? Maria belongs to a Puerto Rican street gang while Tony belongs to the American gang. Both risk everything, including their lives, in pursuit of lasting love.

In the film *Titanic,* a rich girl named Rose battles the pressures of social class and family expectations in order to be with Jack. She even chooses to go down with the ship rather than part from her lover.

I could go on and on. Clearly, *Twilight's* Bella is not the first character in a story to consider life worthless if separated from her beloved. Bella's desire for Edward drives her to ignore feuding clans and life-threatening danger, including the greatest danger, Edward himself. As Bella explains, "About three things I was absolutely positive. First, Edward was a vampire. Second, there was a part of him—and I didn't know how dominant that part might be—that thirsted for my blood. And third, I was unconditionally and irrevocably in love with him."[1]

I'm sure many readers view Bella's reckless abandon as mere melodramatic immaturity. Perhaps. But that doesn't explain why the same idea surfaces in countless other stories or why young lovers scratch and claw their way over every obstacle that stands between them. Throughout history storytellers have reminded us of the mysteriously magnetic force that brings two half-people together as a single whole. These "myths" point us to the very purpose of our existence.

HEALTHY DESIRE

God gave us the gift of romantic attraction for a reason. It is not, as some have suggested, a dirty consequence of the Fall. Adam had "the hots" for Eve long before either ate the forbidden fruit. The two completed one another. The two needed one another to fulfill their destiny as God's image bearers and representatives on earth. The desire Adam felt for Eve is the same desire each of us feel when attracted to a potential mate. Like hunger pangs, the desire reminds us that we were made for intimacy. As C.S. Lewis put it, "Creatures are not born with desires unless satisfaction for those desires exists. A baby feels hunger; well, there is such a thing as food. A duckling wants to swim; well, there is such a thing as water. Men feel sexual desire; well, there is such a thing as sex. If I find in myself a desire which no experience in this world can satisfy, the most probable explanation is that I was made for another world."[2]

Every desire we feel has a healthy, God-intended source for satisfaction. Of course we can try to satisfy healthy desires in an unhealthy manner. When my stomach growls for nourishment, I can pick up an apple. But I can also choose a candy bar. Either will temporarily stop the craving. But one brings health while the other brings fat cells and clogged arteries. In the next chapter we will explore some of the "junk food" found in the *Twilight* romance. Before dwelling on the negative, however, I want to explore the God-given desires that make romantic attraction such a powerful force in human experience.

Have you ever had a crush on someone? There is nothing quite so wonderful and awful; the thrill of their presence—even their voice. You notice everything; how she dresses, the way he walks. The upward or downward curve of an eyebrow can make or ruin your week. Anxious uncertainty hoping they will notice you, perhaps even like you or, someday, love you. Do you remember getting tongue-tied in the middle of an ordinary conversation about some insignificant topic? You so wanted to make a good impression that you made a fool of yourself. At least that's the way it felt.

In order to understand why we have these feelings, we need to go all the way back to the beginning by imagining what it must have been like for Adam and Eve in the Garden of Eden. That part of human history is contained in the first two chapters of the Book of Genesis.

> *So God created man in His own image; in the image of God He created him; male and female He created them. Then God blessed them, and God said to them, "Be fruitful and multiply..."* (Genesis 1:27-28).

God made us with two primary purposes in mind. First, we were made to reflect His image, something we do most fully when two become one in the bond of marriage. Second, we were made to participate in God's ongoing work of creation by filling the earth with more of those made in His image. Of course, we can't fulfill either of these purposes until two single people come together to form a pair. The two halves become one whole and their loving attraction to one another brings forth the life of a third, forth, fifth, etc.

Of course, this can only happen if someone plays matchmaker; which is precisely what happened next.

> *And the Lord God said, "It is not good that man should be alone; I will make him a helper comparable to him." ...and He brought her to the man. And Adam said: "This is now bone of my bones, and flesh*

of my flesh; she shall be called Woman, because she was taken out of Man." Therefore a man shall leave his father and mother and be joined to his wife, and they shall become one flesh. And they were both naked, the man and his wife, and were not ashamed" (Genesis 2:18-25).

In the first ever "blind date," the Lord introduced Adam to Eve. Everything was new to the first couple. It had to be overwhelming, and exhilarating! Basking in the tender care of their Creator, walking hand in hand "in the cool of the day" and enjoying the sights, sounds, smells, and tastes of a virgin world. They must have been like a couple on their first date discovering just how wonderful the other can be.

There is nothing like the early days of romantic love. Intense feelings of attraction overpower every other life priority. You can hardly stand to be away from that special someone. Moments together are like Heaven; moments apart sheer torture. That's because God made us for one another. As we learn from the story of the very first man and woman, intimacy between us is an essential part of what it means to be made in the image of God.

"How could that be?" you may ask. "After all, God does not need anyone else. So why should we?"

Actually, God is no lone ranger. The reason He said, "It is not good that man should be alone" is because not even God exists in solitude. Have you ever heard of the mystery of the Trinity? From the earliest days of the Church, Jesus' followers have affirmed the existence of one God in three distinct persons—God the Father, God the Son, and God the Holy Spirit. Belief in the mystery of the Trinity has been **the** essential doctrine of Christian faith from the very beginning. As the most widely quoted Christian creed explains:

> *We* **believe** *in one* **God**, *the* **Father** *Almighty,* **Maker** *of heaven and earth, and of all things visible and invisible; and in one Lord* **Jesus Christ**, *the Son of God, the Only-begotten, Begotten of the Father before all worlds, Light of Light, Very God of Very God, Begotten, not made; of one essence with the Father, by whom all things were made . . . And we believe in the* **Holy Spirit**, *the Lord, and Giver of Life, Who proceeds from the Father, Who with the Father and the Son together is* **worshipped** *and glorified...*[3]

In short, God is a community of love—an eternal unity of intimacy between the three persons of the Trinity. And it is because we are made in that image that we feel incomplete until intimately joined with another. Even our bodies shout, "I want to unite!" That's why chemical reactions occur when a man and woman become attracted to one another. The desire for marriage and parenthood were hard-coded into human DNA as a reflection of the One whose image we bear.

The Christian Church has described marriage and parenthood as "a communion of persons, a sign and image of the communion of the Father and the Son in the Holy Spirit."[4] It has also explained that sexual intimacy is not something simply biological but "concerns the innermost being of the human person as such. It is realized in a truly human way only if it is an integral part of the love by which a man and woman commit themselves totally to one another until death."[5]

A BREATH OF FRESH AIR

In the *Twilight* series, Bella and Edward ignore the better part of judgment in pursuit of an "eternal union of intimacy." Many consider such young love immature and melodramatic, recognizing that the

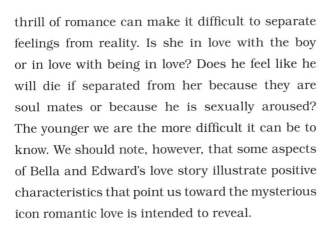
thrill of romance can make it difficult to separate feelings from reality. Is she in love with the boy or in love with being in love? Does he feel like he will die if separated from her because they are soul mates or because he is sexually aroused? The younger we are the more difficult it can be to know. We should note, however, that some aspects of Bella and Edward's love story illustrate positive characteristics that point us toward the mysterious icon romantic love is intended to reveal.

Let's be honest. Fewer and fewer young people in our generation understand or accept such lofty notions of romantic love. To many, waiting until marriage for sexual intimacy has become an outdated, unrealistic notion. The call to remain faithful to one person for an entire lifetime and to partner to raise children seems too much to ask. Once upon a time these expectations were considered healthy and normal. Now they are considered odd. That's why many consider the *Twilight* series a breath of fresh air. The romance between Bella and Edward harkens back to more traditional values because, as fans are quick to point out, they don't sleep together despite the temptation to do so. We'll address the temptation side later. For now, however, I want to take a moment to celebrate some of the honorable characteristics portrayed in this love story.

Drawn to Beauty

Bella repeatedly describes the vampires, especially Edward, as beautiful. She never seems to lose her fascination with those people she calls "devastatingly, inhumanly beautiful."[6] She suggests that Edward looked "more like a Greek god than anyone had a right to"[7] and finds herself despairing that he "was too perfect" so that there could be "no way this godlike creature could be meant for me."[8]

Of course, Edward (along with other boys) also admires the beauty of Bella. It is almost poetic that the author gave her the name *Bella Swan*. Her first name, of Italian and Latin origin, means "beautiful" or "beauty." Her last name, *Swan*, suggests the grace and purity of creation's loveliest bird. Every girl wants to be seen as beautiful. Why? Because deep down they know that they possess swan-like loveliness, even if hidden during the "ugly duckling" adolescent years.

Is such an emphasis on physical beauty healthy? Yes, if we understand the real meaning of beauty.

It has been said that beauty is in the eye of the beholder. On one level, I suppose that's true. From the first time I saw my bride to be, every other woman began to diminish. But on another level, this isn't true. Certainly one "beholder" can appreciate different degrees and types of beauty more than another, but neither determines beauty itself. Plato taught that we see beauty in temporal things because of the existence of an ideal, transcendent beauty. Ultimate beauty—that for which our hearts long—is not in the specific man or woman. Christian philosopher Saint Thomas Aquinas said that "beauty is the participation of the first cause which makes all things beautiful. Indeed, the beauty of a creature is nothing but the likeness of divine beauty participated in things."[9]

In other words, God—the first cause—is ultimate beauty. The people we admire around us only faintly reflect His true beauty, like catching a whiff of a passing woman's perfume. We can like one perfume more than another, but they all share in common the characteristic of sweet, pleasant aroma. Fancy department stores don't sell bottled stench.

The world admired the late Princess Diana because she, perhaps more than most women, reflected the true form of physical beauty. The same can be said of countless other women, and to some degree, of them all. Whether seen in their eyes or their grace or their figure or their hair or their softness or their smile or their legs or in any number of characteristics, women reflect a beauty that echoes true, pure femininity.

It also has been said that beauty is more than skin deep. We admired Mother Teresa because she, perhaps more than most women, reflected the true form of spiritual beauty. Whether seen in her kindness or her maternal nurturing or her selfless diligence or her love for discarded life or her quiet strength, Teresa was an icon of true, pure goodness. She provided a faint reflection of the kind of true, pure goodness God is.

Appreciating the beauty of others is actually a way of admiring God's self-portrait. After all, the Bible says that "God created man in His own image...male and female He created them."[10] So when Bella describes Edward as "god-like" she is not far off! Our draw to beauty ultimately reflects our hunger for God.

Masculine Strength

One of the most dramatic scenes *Twilight* portrays is Edward darting across the parking lot in a flash to put himself between Bella and an oncoming vehicle. She would have been crushed, but instead

finds herself safely shielded behind Edward's out-
stretched arm. The van, rather than Bella, absorbs
the impact of the collision—our first indication that
Edward possesses superhuman strength.

What makes him particularly appealing to Bella
and readers, however, is not his ability to stop an
oncoming automobile or run like the wind. Edward
demonstrates the strength of character to overcome
evil desires, including the desire to drink Bella's
delicious smelling blood. "I wrestled all night," he
told her "while watching you sleep, with the chasm
between what I knew was *right*, moral, ethical, and
what I *wanted*."[11] Virtuous men have historically
disciplined themselves and pursued heroic self-sacrifice rather than cowardly self-indulgence. They
found a sense of meaning in the role of provider
and protector rather than consumer and stalker.
Edward's character symbolizes a man's conscious
decision to abandon the self-centered tendencies of
boyhood and intentionally move toward the self-
sacrificial call of manhood.

Real strength means doing what is hard when
we would rather do what is pleasant. Such strength
defines real masculinity. Nothing is less manly than
the weight-lifter who spends all of his time admiring his own perfectly formed body. True manhood
involves character, courage, and the willingness to

lay down one's life for others in the spirit of the ultimate "man's man" Jesus Christ who "humbled Himself and became obedient to the point of death, even the death of the cross."[12]

For Edward, stopping a van was easy compared to the moment he was forced to muster every ounce of self-control he possesses in order to suck vampire poison out of Bella's arm. Edward hesitates, fearing he might not be able to stop sucking once he begins. But his beloved's life is at stake. So, as Bella describes:

> *Edward's face was drawn. I watched his eyes as the doubt was suddenly replaced with a blazing determination. His jaw tightened. I felt his cool, strong fingers on my burning hand, locking it in place. Then his head bent over it, and his cold lips pressed against my skin* (Twilight, 455-456).

He does find the strength to stop, and in the process saves Bella from a dark fate. That's what real men do.

Feminine Mystique

In addition to his other superhuman abilities, Edward has the unique ability to read minds.

"How does it work—the mind reading thing?" Bella inquired. "Can you read anybody's mind, anywhere?"[13]

For some unexplained reason, however, Edward can't read Bella's mind. And that is a very good thing. You see, a big part of what makes women so intriguing to men is what can't be known or seen. Certainly, men are drawn to a woman's physical beauty. But they are also drawn to something past generations called feminine mystique.

I am not referring to the famous book written by Betty Friedan in the 1960s. I am referring to that special something men have found irresistible since Eve's first shy wink at Adam in the Garden of Eden.

The word *mystique* is borrowed from a French adjective that means mystic. It suggests an air of mystery; meaning something you can observe but can't understand. It also implies reverence as one recognizes that he is in the presence of something wonderfully different. When you couple mystique with feminine, you get the picture of a man staring at a lovely creature who can be observed but not understood.

In our generation the notion of mystique has gone the way of the dinosaurs. Boys don't wonder about feminine charms because those charms are no longer hidden. A boy doesn't need to read a girl's mind since most girls are all too eager to reveal every secret thought and overwhelm boys with a barrage of phone calls, text messages, and online chat sessions that drain away all sense of "mystery" from the relationship.

Every other person around Edward is predictably boring because he can read their minds. Bella, on the other hand, remains a mystery. Her mystique keeps him wondering, which, in turn, makes her interesting.

OBSTACLES

Meyer's books are page turners in large part because readers want to know how this couple will overcome seemingly impossible obstacles in order to fulfill the yearning each has for the other. (Romeo and Juliet had obstacles to overcome, but at least both were human!) Every great love story does the same.

In the classic musical *The Sound of Music*, for example, Maria and Captain Von Trapp face obstacles. She wants to become a nun. He is engaged to someone else. Not to mention the fact each finds the other somewhat irritating. But in the end, love finds a way.

In the 2001 film *Notting Hill* Hugh Grant's character (William Thacker) falls for the breathtaking Anna Scott (played by Julia Roberts). But what hope does he have? She is a glamorous American movie star and he a failing British bookstore owner. She has an explosive temper, a boyfriend, and an army of tabloid journalists following her every move. Can love possibly overcome such enormous hurdles? You bet.

The examples go on and on. Cinderella must overcome an oppressive step-mother and step-sisters. Aladdin must overcome his status as a poor street-rat to win the hand of the lovely princess. And the trash-compacting WALL-E faces serious technological limitations if he hopes to mate with the futuristic EVE. Still, in each and every story, love overcomes every obstacle in order to unite. Each and every one of these love stories points to a larger, true tale.

"Suppose there was a king who loved a humble

maiden." So begins a parable written by Christian philosopher Soren Kierkegaard illustrating how God might overcome the infinite distance between fallen humanity and a holy God. There are only two options. Either the maiden must elevate herself to royalty—an impossible task—or the king must find a way to lower himself in order to win her heart. But the king's position commands submission whether she loves him or not. So he must approach the maiden in disguise—wooing her heart in common attire lest she fear his position rather than love his heart.

In the Old Testament Book of Song of Solomon, the king of Israel pursues a humble maiden. Her beauty hidden by the effects of poverty, hard work, and cruel brothers—the maiden resembled Cinderella. Unnoticed and unappreciated, she was condemned to a life of empty days and lonely nights.

But one day, a handsome young shepherd entered the picture. Showering the maiden with admiration and flattery, he made her blush in self-conscious embarrassment. But he also stole her heart. For the first time ever, someone thought her beautiful and worthy of pursuit. Though she didn't know his name, she fell in love with his strong presence and gentle kindness.

As the story unfolds, we discover that the shepherd lad is really the king in disguise. Having humbled himself in order to win her heart, he was unwilling to reveal his true identity until their wedding day. As a result, the king entered marriage certain that she married him out of affection rather than duty. Had he met the maiden in the splendor of the throne room, he would never have known whether she truly loved him. By approaching her in disguise, he learned that she did indeed love his heart, not just fear his position.

By becoming a man, the King of Heaven left His eternal throne room and approached us in a manner that showed we could love His heart, rather than just fear His position. He extended His hand to ours in many ways; by calling us to abandon the road we were traveling—and the death we were living. He asked us to abandon all other "lovers" to be exclusively His. In the process, our hearts discover the warmth and thrill of true love.

God made us for intimacy with Himself. The Old Testament Scriptures actually say that He invites His people to become His "bride."

> *I remember the devotion of your youth,*
> *how as a bride you loved me and followed*

me through the desert (Jeremiah 2:2
NIV).

In the New Testament, Christ is described as the
Bridegroom and the Church as His Bride.

> *"For this reason a man will leave his
> father and mother and be united to his
> wife, and the two will become one flesh."
> This is a profound mystery—but I am
> talking about Christ and the church*
> (Ephesians 5:31-32 NIV).

Our romantic inclinations drive us toward the
life-long beauty of marriage. They also point us to
our ultimate purpose of "marrying" God. As author
Christopher West put it:

> *Everyone knows the "magnetic pull" of
> erotic desire. This basic human longing
> for union, in fact, is the most concrete link
> in every human heart with "that man
> who lived two thousand years ago." For
> all human longing, when purified, leads
> us to Christ, and none more so than the
> longing to unite with an "other" in sexual
> embrace. "For this reason...the two
> become one flesh." For what reason? To*

> reveal, proclaim, and anticipate the union
> of Christ and the Church.[14]

The bad news, however, is that we are fallen men and women prone toward mistakes and sin. So we often twist the healthy hunger of romance into something ugly and detrimental. "Sin's tactic," adds West "is simply to 'twist' and 'disorient' our desire for heaven...the sexual confusion so prevalent in our world and in our own hearts is nothing but the human desire for heaven gone berserk."[15]

As we will explore in the next chapter, Bella Swan goes slightly "berserk" at times when her hunger for love turns into a lust thirst.

Chapter Five

Lust Thirst

"I know love and lust don't always keep the same company." —Edward Cullen

As we discovered in the last chapter, romantic desire is healthy and an essential part of our humanity when experienced as God intended. Sadly, however, we can twist what is pure and beautiful into something ugly and destructive. So we ask—does the *Twilight* series handle romance in a manner that provides young readers nourishing fruit or an unhealthy candy bar?

In short, it does both. On the positive side, Edward and Bella resist the temptation to have sex throughout most of the series. The bad news is that countless girls, many still in elementary school, immerse themselves in a story that evokes strong erotic images and emotions. *Time* magazine described the sexuality of the stories like this:

> It is the rare vampire novel that isn't about sex on some level, and the Twilight books are no exception. What makes Meyer's books so distinctive is that they're about the erotics of abstinence. Their tension comes from prolonged, superhuman acts of self-restraint.... It's never quite clear whether Edward wants to sleep with Bella or rip her throat out or both, but he wants something, and he wants it bad, and you feel it all the more because he never gets it. That's the power of the Twilight books: they're squeaky, geeky clean on the surface, but right below it, they are absolutely, deliciously filthy.[1]

I must agree. Throughout the series Bella Swan seems eager to lose her virginity without a single moral qualm. Just consider the progressive intensity of her relationship with Edward in scenes that surface throughout the book.

***Twilight*, Chapter 11**: Bella and Edward sit

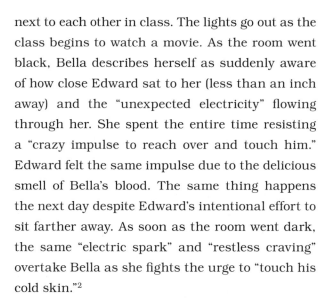

next to each other in class. The lights go out as the class begins to watch a movie. As the room went black, Bella describes herself as suddenly aware of how close Edward sat to her (less than an inch away) and the "unexpected electricity" flowing through her. She spent the entire time resisting a "crazy impulse to reach over and touch him." Edward felt the same impulse due to the delicious smell of Bella's blood. The same thing happens the next day despite Edward's intentional effort to sit farther away. As soon as the room went dark, the same "electric spark" and "restless craving" overtake Bella as she fights the urge to "touch his cold skin."[2]

Twilight, Chapter 13: Edward describes himself as "the world's best predator" because everything about him causes Bella (and presumably other women) to become irresistibly attracted to his voice, face, body, and smell. Making matters even more challenging, Bella possesses unique characteristics that Edward finds difficult to resist. In fact, he admits, "I crave your company too much to do what I should." He should stay away from her to avoid the temptation of Bella's aroma which he describes as "exactly my brand of heroin." Rather than keep their distance due to the dangers, however, they let the relationship progress very quickly. After an exciting run into the solitude of the woods, Edward decides to test his own self-control by kissing Bella. What neither anticipated was the sexual desires that kiss would spark in her. "Blood boiled under my skin, burned my lips. My breath came in a wild gasp. My fingers knotted in his hair, clutching him to me. My lips parted as I breathed in his heady scent."[3]

Twilight, Chapter 14: Because Edward doesn't sleep at night, he makes a habit of staying in Bella's room to watch her sleep. Excited about having him in her room, Bella goes into her bathroom to shower and change—wishing she had thought to bring her Victoria's Secret pajamas instead of a holey t-shirt and sweat pants. Edward describes the internal wrestling match he experiences while watching Bella sleep between "what I knew was right, moral, ethical, and what I wanted." When he admits that love and lust "don't always keep the same company" Bella responds "They do for me."[4]

New Moon, Chapter 2: Edward tucks Bella into her bed and lays down next to her on top of the blanket. Curling up under his arm, she asks what he is thinking about. When he admits "I was thinking about right and wrong" Bella feels a chill tingle along her spine—so she asks Edward to kiss her. "You're greedy tonight." He responds

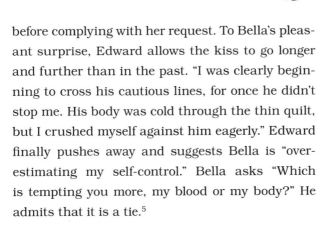

before complying with her request. To Bella's pleasant surprise, Edward allows the kiss to go longer and further than in the past. "I was clearly beginning to cross his cautious lines, for once he didn't stop me. His body was cold through the thin quilt, but I crushed myself against him eagerly." Edward finally pushes away and suggests Bella is "over-estimating my self-control." Bella asks "Which is tempting you more, my blood or my body?" He admits that it is a tie.[5]

***New Moon,* Chapter 23**: After a prolonged separation, Bella and Edward re-ignite their passion for one another. His kiss is described as less careful than others "which suited me just fine" admits Bella. She kissed him back with her "heart pounding out a jagged, disjointed rhythm while my breathing turned to panting" and she could "feel his marble body against every line of mine."[6]

***Eclipse,* Chapter 2**: Bella admits that she would like to spend the majority of her time kissing Edward because nothing in life compared to the experience of kissing his "cool lips, marble hard but always so gentle, moving with mine." So she continues to pursue him, causing Edward to press her tightly against himself. "Even through his sweater, his skin was cold enough to make me shiver—it was a shiver of pleasure..." Once again, Edward loosens their embrace to resist temptation, but she "crushed myself closer, molding myself to the shape of him" and used her tongue to trace the curve of his lower lip. As they part, she senses Edward's frustration with yet another tempting moment. "I'd say I'm sorry," she responds "but I'm not."[7]

***Eclipse*, Chapter 8:** Bella is staying at Edward's house for security purposes, sleeping in his room. She awakes one night to discover he is lying on the bed beside her. "I could almost taste the sweetness of reunion in the air" as she "reached out for him, found his hands in the darkness, and pulled myself closer to him...My lips searched, hunting along his throat, to his chin, till I finally found his lips." Then Edward made his move, as Bella describes it: "His hand curved around my elbow, moving slowly down my arm, across my ribs and over my waist, tracing along my hip and down my leg, around my knee." He eventually finds her calf and pulls her leg up to hitch it around his hip. "I stopped breathing." Bella admits. "This wasn't the kind of thing he usually allowed. Despite his cold hands, I felt suddenly warm. His lips moved in the hollow at the base of my throat." They stop short of going all the way, which frustrates Bella. "If we're not going to get carried away, what's the point?" Edward

explains that to do so would be too dangerous. To which she replied "I like danger."[8]

***Eclipse*, Chapter 14:** After another tempting moment between Bella and Edward, she reflects upon her intense desire for him to turn her into a vampire so they could be together forever. "I liked the idea that *his* lips would be the last good thing I would feel...I wanted *his* venom to poison my system. It would make me belong to him in a tangible, quantifiable way."[9]

***Eclipse*, Chapter 20**: In her most overt attempt to seduce Edward into having sex, Bella senses his defenses weaken. She describes him as "less guarded than usual," causing her to think that perhaps "getting what I wanted would not be as difficult as I'd expected it to be." When Edward resists, Bella goes even further. "My hands were slightly shaky as I unlocked my arms from around his neck. My fingers slid down his neck to the collar of his shirt. The trembling didn't help as I tried to hurry to undo the buttons before he stopped me." As she begins to unbutton her own blouse, Bella feels a "thrill of victory" that gave her a "strange high" that made her "feel powerful." They don't go all the way, but Bella does make it clear that the "one thing" she wants from Edward is sexual intercourse. In a moment of role reversal from the typical scenario, he says they should wait until they are married before having sex—which makes Bella very upset.[10]

As I mentioned earlier, one of the things *Twilight* fans celebrate about the series is the fact Bella and Edward avoid pre-marital sex. In light of the fact many vampire love story novels are intensely erotic and sexualized, I suppose that is commendable. On the other hand, these and other scenes make it clear that Edward and Bella would have gone all the way if not for his self-control. Edward even refers to concern over breaking the biblical commandment against infidelity—even though he has already broken other biggies like "You shall not murder." But we should note the primary reason Edward resists temptation. He fears that Bella's body and blood will drive him mad to the point he will accidentally kill her.

Unfortunately, Bella shows no signs of maturity or self-restraint at all. She seems to have bought into the notion that intense feelings for a guy are reason enough to sleep with him. She even wears the hat typically worn by the guy—pushing to have sex before marriage as a test of his love.

As much as we may want to sympathize with Bella, we can't overlook the fact that she lacks

moral fiber and allows herself to become so caught up in the passion of romance that she becomes the temptress.

Consider how one book of ancient wisdom described such a woman while giving advice to virtuous men:

> *For the lips of an immoral woman drip honey, and her mouth is smoother than oil; but in the end she is bitter as wormwood, sharp as a two-edged sword. Her feet go down to death, her steps lay hold of hell... Remove your way far from her, and do not go near the door of her house, lest you give your honor to others, and your years to the cruel one... when your flesh and your body are consumed* (Proverbs 5:3-11).

❧

> *...and he took the path to her house, in the twilight, in the evening, in the black and dark night. And there a woman met him, with the attire of a harlot, and a crafty heart...So she caught him and kissed him; with an impudent face she*

said to him...Come, let us take our fill of love until morning; let us delight ourselves with love...With her enticing speech she caused him to yield, with her flattering lips she seduced him...Her house is the way to hell, descending to the chambers of death (Proverbs 7:8-27).

Considering the parallels between what the Scriptures call a "crafty harlot" and the actions of Bella Swan, she is hardly the kind of girl we want our elementary-aged daughters celebrating or emulating.

"But *Twilight* is a series of fictional love stories, not a moral instruction manual." That's right. And yet, as we explored in chapters one and two, we often embrace the "truth" presented in fiction more readily than we do religious training. Good stories have always portrayed the realities of temptation and the internal conflicts inherent in romantic relationships. But they also provide a moral compass that shows the downside of sin. Bella becomes angry over her inability to seduce Edward. But she never demonstrates remorse for trying to seduce him. On the contrary, young readers will glean from her all of the wrong messages—including:

- Even good girls are eager to have sex before marriage.

- It is OK to tempt a guy sexually. You can rely upon his self-restraint to avoid risky behavior.

- When caught up in the passion of the moment, go with your feelings.

- Sex and marriage are not necessarily linked.

Again, the erotic tone of the *Twilight* series is quite tame when compared to many romance novels and vampire stories. But this series has found its way into the eager hands of very young girls. One of the things that makes a story so influential is our tendency to identify with the feelings, values, and choices of the main character. In this case, the main character is a teenage girl who can't control her own feelings and throws herself at a boy she knows wants her body and her blood.

What Christopher West described as "sexual confusion gone berserk" happens when we separate erotic desire from its intended context of marriage. Romantic love is intended to point us toward our ultimate purpose of selfless, committed intimacy. So what happens when we pursue self-centered sexual intimacy with no commitment? In short, we fit the traditional role of vampires—those who drain the life from others for their own gratification.

In the typical vampire romance story, the vampire is driven by lust thirst. In the *Twilight* series, by contrast, Edward desires a legitimate, committed marital union with Bella. Yet Bella reveals an odd tension between her desire to have sex with Edward and her intense aversion to the idea of marriage. As a result, we see a role reversal. Bella behaves more like a vampire than Edward. She has bought into a cultural lie and, as a result, seems eager to discard the real thing for a cheap imitation.

Consider Bella's reaction to the thought of walking down the aisle:

New Moon, Chapter 24: When Edward suggests Bella marry him before they sleep together, she displays an almost irrational distaste for the idea. "Look, marriage isn't exactly that high on my list of priorities, you know?" She acknowledges she prefers the risk of eternal damnation to getting married because marriage was "sort of the kiss of death for Renee and Charlie."[11] She blames

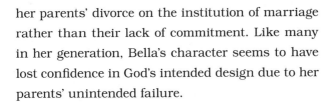

her parents' divorce on the institution of marriage rather than their lack of commitment. Like many in her generation, Bella's character seems to have lost confidence in God's intended design due to her parents' unintended failure.

***Eclipse,* Chapter 12:** Trying to explain her reluctance to get married to Edward, Bella sheepishly admits that she never saw herself as "that girl," the girl who got married right out of high school like some "small-town hick who got knocked up by her boy friend." She worried what people would think since she was only 18. Smart, responsible, mature people don't do that. "In my mind," she continues, "marriage and eternity are not mutually exclusive or mutually inclusive concepts." She would rather "go with the times" than live by values of the past.[12]

***Eclipse,* Chapter 20**: Bella becomes infuriated by Edward's stipulation that the two get married before having sex by calling marriage a "stupid" and "ridiculous" thing. She explains that marriage is a stretch for her, so she won't give in to it unless she gets something in return. "I'll give you what you want." promised Edward. "I'll marry you." To him, marriage and sex go together. To her, marriage is an unreasonable request. The two acknowledge they are in a bit of a role reversal since guys usually push for sex and girls typically want to marry. "Maybe it wouldn't bug me so much," she admits "if I hadn't been raised to shudder at the thought of marriage."[13] Sadly, Bella does not want what is typical. She wants much less.

Too Easily Pleased

What happens when a virtuous girl loses her purity by indulging sexual desires outside the exciting and protective confines of a committed marriage relationship? She becomes a parable for the shame and defilement of every other sin.

A tearful young woman takes a long shower, trying to wash away the shame she feels after her first illicit encounter. Be it the abuse of rape or voluntary infidelity, the loss of sexual innocence makes us feel dirty, violated, ashamed. But that same girl will have a very different reaction after a year of prostitution. A cold stare tells you her heart is resigned to the shame that now defines her existence. A seductive glance suggests an acquired taste for erotic pleasures. Dark shadows under her eyes and deep facial lines invade the soft, graceful beauty she once possessed. And loud, brazen laughter overtakes the gentle, pretty smile that was so charming just twelve months earlier.

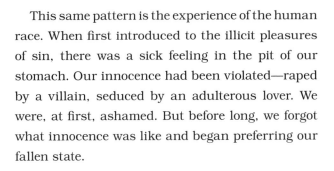

This same pattern is the experience of the human race. When first introduced to the illicit pleasures of sin, there was a sick feeling in the pit of our stomach. Our innocence had been violated—raped by a villain, seduced by an adulterous lover. We were, at first, ashamed. But before long, we forgot what innocence was like and began preferring our fallen state.

The sad reality of the Fall is that we now crave that which should make us cry. The human race has been living in bondage to sin for so long that we cannot even remember the thrilling excitement and passion found in purity. Celebrating our addictions, we view them as keys of liberation rather than chains of enslavement.

In C.S. Lewis' fictitious series of letters between two demons, the elder Screwtape advises his nephew Wormwood on how to use God's invention of pleasure against us.

> *Never forget that when we are dealing with any pleasure in its healthy and normal and satisfying form, we are, in a sense, on the Enemy's ground. I know we have won many a soul through pleasure. All the same, it is His invention, not ours...Hence we always try to*

work away from the natural condition of any pleasure to that in which it is least natural, least redolent of its Maker, and least pleasurable. An ever increasing craving for an ever diminishing pleasure is the formula.[14]

Our new "lover" has twisted the gift of desire into an affliction, driving us to things that kill rather than fulfill.

My bones have no soundness because of my sin. My guilt has overwhelmed me like a burden too heavy to bear. My wounds fester and are loathsome because of my sinful folly (Psalm 38:3b-5 NIV).

❧

When you were slaves to sin, you were free from the control of righteousness. What benefit did you reap at that time from the things you are now ashamed of? Those things result in death! (Romans 6:20-21 NIV)

❧

> *But each one is tempted when, by his own evil desire, he is dragged away and enticed. Then, after desire has conceived, it gives birth to sin; and sin, when it is full-grown, gives birth to death* (James 1:14-15 NIV).

This is the reality of every person born on earth. We all experience the enticement and enslavement of sin—pulling us deeper into the abyss of self-gratification. "Ever increasing craving for an ever diminishing pleasure." But, unlike Lucifer, we are made in God's image. Our hearts were made to experience more.

So is our desire for romantic intimacy a blessing or a curse? What do they tell us about the "more" we were made for? "Our Lord finds our desires not too strong, but too weak" wrote C.S. Lewis. "We are half-hearted creatures, fooling around with drink and sex and ambition when infinite joy is offered us, like an ignorant child who wants to go on making mud pies in a slum because he cannot imagine what is meant by the offer of a holiday at the sea. We are far too easily pleased."[15]

The Scriptures tell us that God is love. So as those created in God's image, we are hard-wired for a love that finds its source and aim in Him. We fully live when we fully love. And we fully love when we, like Christ, give ourselves away.

Love is central to what it means to be human. We were created male and female, two halves of a whole. That's why love's magnetic force irresistibly and incessantly draws us toward that special someone who can become our completing opposite; our other half.

This idea is woven into the fabric of every Christian tradition. The late John Paul II, for example, said that man "becomes the image of God not so much in the moment of solitude as in the moment of communion."[16] Why? Because, as the catechism explains, "God who created man out of love calls him to love—the fundamental and innate vocation of every human being. For man is created in the image and likeness of God who is himself love. Since God created man and woman, their mutual love becomes an image of the absolute and unfailing love with which God loves man."[17]

The Scriptures are filled with marital imagery, describing Israel as God's wife and the Church Christ's Bride. Protestant believers routinely celebrate the spiritual significance of romantic love—including the opening words of every wedding ceremony: "Dearly beloved, we are gathered together here in the sight of God...to join this Man and this Woman in holy Matrimony; which is an honorable estate, instituted of God, *signifying unto us the mystical union that is between Christ and his Church.*"[18]

Our attraction to one another is intended to yank us out of self-focused isolation into the kind of intimacy that reflects God's communion with His beloved. With us. That's why the desire for romantic union is imprinted on, programmed into, and seeded within our very souls. It's the reason all of us yearn to meet and marry that special someone.

Whether we find true love or ache from its absence, whether we treat sex as a gift or a game—our love lives drive us toward or away from God. The forks encountered along love's path literally lead to Heaven's highest joys or hell's deepest miseries; a dream come true or a living nightmare. That's why the headlines of history, art, pop-culture, and family photos all shout a common truth; romantic love defines our existence—for better or worse.

On the whole, Bella's relationship with Edward does affirm the deep love hunger of humanity and manages to overcome the temptation of premarital lust. But it does so in spite of Bella's irresponsible choices creating several very close calls!

Chapter Six

Soul Destiny

What if I could be a good vampire right away?
—Bella Swan

What does it mean to be a good person? Are some of us destined for eternal joy while others are condemned to eternal damnation? These questions underlie much of the drama that unfolds throughout the four books of the *Twilight* series. They also permeate the history of philosophy, art, literature, and religious discourse. No matter where you poke the human experience you hit a nerve called ethics and morality. That's because deep down we all suspect that choices in this life influence the possibility of reward or punishment in the afterlife.

Bella Swan and Edward Cullen are no exception. Both reflect upon life's ultimate questions as they wrestle with past and present choices.

Religious themes emerge early in their relationship. "I decided as long as I was going to hell," Edward explained to Bella "I might as well do it thoroughly."[1] Half kidding, he hints at one of Edward's most haunting questions. Does he have a soul? And if so, is that soul damned to hell?

Edward knows himself vulnerable to the tempting allure of evil. Early in their relationship he sees Bella as "some kind of demon, summoned straight from my own personal hell to ruin me" because the aroma of her skin drove him mad. The first time they were forced to sit beside one another in class, he admits, "I thought of a hundred different ways to lure you from the room with me, to get you alone."[2]

Knowing his own weakness for human blood, Edward fears his own capacity for murder. He repeatedly warns Bella of how dangerous it is for her to spend time with him. Once upon a time, after all, Edward had taken the lives of human beings. About ten years after he had been turned into a vampire, Edward admits to Bella, he grew tired of suppressing his appetite for human blood and gave up "abstinence" to enter a season of killing. He even tried to apply a sense of morality to his murders by passing over the innocent to pursue only evil people. "Because I knew the thoughts of my prey," he explained that he, "followed a murderer down a dark alley where he stalked a young girl—if I saved her, then surely I wasn't so terrible."[3]

This theme resurfaces throughout the *Twilight* series as Edward seems tortured by the recognition of his own dark nature. A nature he worries will pull Bella down with him—especially when she says she wants to barter her soul by becoming a vampire. Edward wonders why Bella would be "so eager for eternal damnation."[4]

Clearly Edward takes the notion of Heaven and hell seriously. Bella, on the other hand, does not. Infuriated by Edward's old-fashioned beliefs, Bella proclaims that she doesn't care about her soul. "You can have my soul. I don't want it without you—it's yours already!"[5]

Bella insists that Edward does indeed have a soul. "It seemed silly that this fact—the existence of his soul—had ever been in question, even if he was a vampire. He had the most beautiful soul...."[6]

"I know you believe I have a soul," Edward tells Bella "but I'm not entirely convinced on that point."[7]

One thing he is convinced on, however, is that he refuses to do anything that might cause Bella to lose hers.

That's why Edward repeatedly resists the temptation to sleep with Bella, even after she mocks his old-fashioned values and accuses him of trying to protect his own virtue. "No, silly girl," he retorts "I'm trying to protect yours." Why? Because he believes she still has a shot at Heaven if she follows the right rules of conduct.

Edward acknowledges that despite committing murder, theft, lying, and coveting—he has managed to keep himself sexually pure, which might count for something. But Bella has a pretty clean record which he refuses to tarnish. He won't mess up her chances in the afterlife. "Now, of course, it might be too late for me, even if you are right about my soul...I'll be damned—no pun intended—if I'll let them keep you out, too."[8]

Despite such a flippant attitude toward the afterlife, however, Bella still worries about right and wrong, good and evil. When she researches rumors about the possibility Edward was a vampire, for example, Bella scours the Internet to learn all she can on the subject—including a whole lot of frightening stuff. "It was a relief" she confesses "that one myth among hundreds" claimed the existence of "good vampires."⁹

Even though she might dismiss Edward's moral sensibilities, she desperately wants to see him as a good person, even going so far as to agree to follow his rules because "your soul is far, far too important to me to take chances with."¹⁰ She also takes comfort in the fact that Carlisle believes Edward has a soul and a shot at Heaven, even if Edward does not.

So the world of *Twilight* created in the imagination of Stephenie Meyer includes several realities rooted in our real world; that there is a moral code to respect and that there is an afterlife to anticipate.

GOOD MONSTERS

Do vampires have souls? Is it possible for a monster to find redemption, or at least retain part of his or her humanity? Even though Edward asks such questions about himself, he can't escape the slight hope of his possible redemption.

In the year 1918 Edward lay dying in a hospital bed when a doctor named Carlisle Cullen realized the teenage boy had no chance of surviving the Spanish influenza. So in Edward's words, "Carlisle saved me."[11] How? Well, Carlisle was himself a vampire—so he "saved" the boy from natural death by turning him into a vampire. Thus, Edward became the first in Carlisle's "family" of vampires.

On several occasions in the story they suggest that brutal serial killings are carried out by vampires rather than humans. "Monsters are not a joke," says Edward in response to a headline about mass killings. "You'd be surprised, Bella, at how often my kind are the source behind the horrors in your human news...The existence of monsters results in monstrous consequences."[12]

What kind of consequences? The direct result, of course, would be lifeless corpses. But the idea goes further, touching upon the consequences of personal hatred. At certain points in the story, various characters see the monster of life-stealing selfishness in themselves. It surfaces whenever Edward tries to warn Bella to stay away because he is a dangerous creature, "You don't care if I'm a monster? If I'm not human?"[13] As well as brief glimpses of his self-loathing; "I don't *want* to be a monster."[14]

And Edward is not alone in his regrets. One of his vampire "brothers" named Jasper connects his murderous past to a monstrous self-perception.

"In so many years of slaughter and carnage, I'd lost nearly all of my humanity. I was undeniably a nightmare, a monster of the grisliest kind."[15]

In a few rare moments, even Bella recognizes tendencies in herself that tilt her in the direction of a monster—such as when she realizes she has been taking advantage of Jacob. "If I wasn't mean—and greedy, too," she reflects, "I would tell him I didn't want to be friends and walk away. It was wrong to try to keep my friend when that would hurt him."[16] And later, she begins to see correlation between the life-draining blood-thirst of vampires and the life-stealing self-centeredness of her own vampiric personality. "I wondered if I was a monster. Not the kind that he thought he was, but the real kind. The kind that hurt people. The kind that had no limits when it came to what they wanted."[17]

And what is the key difference between a monster and a hero? Put simply, whether one destroys or protects human life and dignity.

Vampire lore depicts self-gratifying monsters draining the life from human beings to satisfy their own blood lust. Carlisle, by contrast, is portrayed as humane and compassionate. He never infects anyone "who had another choice" so he is considered more heroic savior than villainous devil. In fact, Carlisle becomes a sort of redeemer for other vampires—giving them hope that they too might turn from evil to good.

The Cullen clan, unlike other vampires, restrict themselves to a diet of animal blood. That's why they call themselves "vegetarians." This is possible because Carlisle learned and passed along the art of self-discipline.

"When he knew what he had become" Edward explains "he rebelled against it." At first he rebelled by trying to destroy himself. But another option emerged. Carlisle attacked a herd of deer, causing him to realize "there was an alternative to being the vile monster he feared... Over the next months his new philosophy was born. He could exist without being a demon. He found himself again."

What did he find? His old humanity. More than that, he discovered an enhanced humanity—like a mild-mannered stiff turned mighty superhero. Vampires don't need sleep, so Carlisle spent his nights studying music, science, and medicine. In the process he "found his calling, his penance, in that, in saving human lives."[18]

In other words, Carlisle showed the path from evil to good through the redemptive power of self-discipline. A path that disciples such as Edward and his "siblings" chose to follow also under Carlisle's mentorship.

Bella described him well. "The vampire who wanted to be good—who ran around saving people's lives so he wouldn't be a monster."[19] She also asks of herself, "What if, like Carlisle, I never killed a single person? What if I could be a good vampire right away?"[20]

THE GOOD WE WANT TO DO

Carlisle discovered the alternative path of self-control, freeing him from the damnation of a monster's existence. Edward does likewise, prompting Bella's admiration. "I still don't understand how you can work so hard to resist what you...are." Apparently, she bought into the commonly held notion that one is condemned to live out whatever propensity he finds within, even when that propensity might be self-destructive. Edward disagrees, explaining, "just because we've been...dealt a certain hand...it doesn't mean we can't choose to rise above—to conquer the boundaries of a destiny that none of us wanted. To try to retain whatever essential humanity we can."[21]

I think the apostle Paul would relate to our vampire friends. In a letter he wrote to Christians in Rome, we discover that this early saint wrestled with a similar dilemma. Paul wanted to gain self-control and behave properly. But his propensity toward evil kept pulling him back into a monstrous existence.

"For what I am doing, I do not understand," he admits. "For what I will to do, that I do not practice; but what I hate, that I do." You can hear the torment in Paul's voice as he confesses his internal battle with sin. A battle, by the way, he admits to losing. "For the good that I will to do, I do not do; but the evil I will not to do, that I practice...O wretched man that I am! Who will deliver me from this body of death?" (Romans 7:15,24).

Edward's pep-talk to Paul might go something like this, "I wasn't sure if I was strong enough...And while there was still that possibility that I might be...overcome...I was susceptible. Until I made up my mind that I was strong enough...Mind over matter."[22] After all, that's what he said when asked whether he was still dangerous.

Like the "good" vampires of *Twilight*, the apostle Paul recognized the downward pull of evil within his nature and "willed" himself to overcome ("for to will is present with me"). Unlike Carlisle and Edward, however, Paul admits that he can't defeat the dark impulse toward vampiric selfishness ("but how to perform what is good I do not find").[23]

Is Paul's problem, as Edward might suggest, simply that he lacks enough self-control? Is the path to becoming "good" only available to those few who have the willpower to apply "mind over matter" when it comes to dark impulses? Or, returning to the question that began this chapter, is a soul's destiny linked to good over bad behavior?

Surprisingly, no it isn't. At least if we believe Paul, the apostle who explained Christianity better than anyone else. Yes, personal choices are important—and we should resist our downward urges to reach toward our higher calling. But our most disciplined effort will not, in and of itself, make us good—or assure we reach Heaven over hell.

Do you remember Paul's question in reaction to his own sin? "Who will deliver me from this body of death?" He proceeds to give an answer. "For what the law [think self-disciplined obedience] could not do in that it was weak through the flesh [think our natural bent], God did by sending His own Son in the likeness of sinful flesh, on account of sin: He condemned sin in the flesh that the righteous requirement of the law might be fulfilled in us who do not walk according to the flesh but according to the Spirit."[24]

What is Paul saying? That no one, regardless of how well-intentioned or disciplined they may be, can become "good" by their own efforts. It had to be accomplished on our behalf and imparted to us by the only One capable of redeeming a human soul. Earlier in the same letter Paul explained that "the wages of sin is death, but the gift of God is eternal life in Christ Jesus our Lord."[25] He also celebrates the source of our good fortune when he wrote "But God demonstrates His own love toward us, in that while we were still sinners, Christ died for us."[26]

Can a monster become a hero? Yes. But only because the true hero of history (Jesus Christ) sacrificed Himself on our behalf—rendering impotent the shape-shifting monster of history (satan) in his efforts "seeking whom he may devour."[27]

Heroic self-sacrifice is the key to redemption rather than heroic self-discipline. Human depravity (the "monster" within us) is like an armed hand grenade tossed into a crowd of men and women. Those who grab the grenade trying to "will" their own safety soon discover the fallacy of "mind over matter." Christianity recognizes that someone else (Jesus Christ) needed to throw His own body on top of the grenade to rescue the rest of us from its destructive blast. In short, God became human in order to accomplish what no other human could do for himself—no matter how much willpower we may muster.

I should note that Meyer's Mormon theology carries a very different connotation than orthodox Christianity on this point. Mormons consider Christian denominations in error because we believe in the mystery of the Trinity—one God in three persons (Father, Son, and Holy Spirit). This doctrine has been an essential belief of all Christians ever since the early church. Joseph Smith, founder of the Mormon religion, taught that Jesus Christ, God the Father, and the Holy Ghost were "three distinct personages and three Gods."[28]

Orthodox Christianity also teaches that God became a man through the incarnation of Jesus Christ in order to redeem humanity. Traditional Mormonism, in contrast, teaches that God was once a man who modeled for the rest of us the path toward our own godhood. In the words of Mormon Apostle James Talmadge, "We believe in a God who is...a Being who has attained His exalted state by a path which now His children are permitted to follow...the church proclaims the eternal truth: 'as man is, God once was; as God is, man may be.'[29] Part of that path includes self-restraint and discipline, so it is not surprising this theme plays a prominent part in the path of redemption for Meyer's vampires.

DESTINED FOR JOY

In the final book, *Breaking Dawn*, Bella Swan finally realizes the long yearned for "destiny" that brings her life meaning and joy. I, for one, welcomed the change in Bella since she seemed rather self-consumed, manipulative, and moody throughout the first three books. What brought about the dramatic change in Bella? Two words: self-sacrifice.

Bella dreaded her wedding because, in her words, "I just couldn't reconcile a staid, respectable, dull concept like *husband* with my concept of Edward."[30] But they did get married, after which she found that a husband is anything but boring. They experienced an exotic honeymoon on an isolated island. Like every virgin couple discovering the excitement of sex, they had to go slow and learn—especially since Edward knew he could easily ruin the marriage by unintentionally killing his bride. But they figured things out, and Bella quickly overcame her aversion to marriage.

Entering into the bliss of marital intimacy awakened Bella to just how wonderful being human can be. She began to rethink her desire to become a vampire, hoping to spend more time experiencing a fulfilled humanity. But that changed when what she assumed to be food poisoning turned out to be pregnancy. Vampires aren't supposed to be able to have children. But then, vampires don't typically marry human beings.

The baby grew very quickly inside Bella's womb—telling them this was no ordinary child. Edward reacts immediately, frightened by the possibility the "fetus" was a life-draining monster who would kill his beloved wife. He wants to rush her to Carlisle to have the baby removed and killed. "We're going to get that thing out before it can hurt any part of you,"[31] he reacts.

Bella, revealing a maturity and grace previously hidden, sees it very differently. "From that first little touch, the whole world shifted...It was more like my heart had grown, swollen up to twice its size in a moment...Children, in the abstract, had never appealed to me...This child, Edward's child, was a whole different story. I wanted him like I wanted air to breathe. Not a choice—a necessity."[32]

In a dramatic portrayal of heroic self-sacrifice,

Bella insists upon carrying the child to term even though the baby grows by draining life from its mother's failing body. Finally, after weeks of suffering and deterioration, the baby is born. But it is clear that Bella will not survive the experience, so Edward quickly injects his own venom into her heart in hopes of saving her as Carlisle had saved him on his own death bed.

Bella got her wish to become a vampire. The price for achieving this destiny, however, was entering the valley of death to give her child life.

Bella describes her journey through that valley as holding "the blackness of nonexistence at bay by inches" and the sufferings as a timeless "fiery torture" that made her plead for death as she endured "one infinite moment of pain." But she knew her own death would take the life of her child, so she went from "being tied to the stake as I burned" to "gripping that stake to hold myself in the fire."[33]

And so, in a surprising twist of fate with profoundly spiritual implications, Bella found her life by losing it.

"I was staring at the most beautiful face in the world...reminding me of the moment when the blackness had almost won, when there was nothing in the world left to hold on to. Nothing strong enough to pull me through the crushing darkness...I'd been right all along. She was worth the fight."[34]

And so the Christian theme of heroic self-sacrifice enters the back door of the story. All of the previous emphasis upon "mind over matter" and "self-discipline" pales in comparison to Bella willingly laying down her life for another. An act, interestingly, that gives birth to a child who serves a messiah-like role by bringing peace to warring factions and by uniting age-old enemies in common purpose against mutual destruction.

Bella believes she has finally realized her soul's destiny. "It was like I had been born to be a vampire...I had found my true place in the world, the place I fit, the place I shined."[35] In language evoking of Heaven-like joys found in the gifts of marriage and family, the birth of this special child also brings about the rebirth of Bella Swan. She becomes a new person—very different from her prior self.

No longer fragile, she becomes strong. On the honeymoon, for example, Edward accidentally bruises his weak, human bride. After becoming a vampire, Bella's strength surpasses all of the Cullens'.

No longer moody, she becomes happy. "It would be hard to find someone less sad than I am now...Not many people get every single thing they want, plus all the things they didn't think to ask for, in the same day."[36]

No longer self-centered, her life becomes about others. "I was euphoric the vast majority of the time." Why? "The days were not long enough for me to get my fill of adoring my daughter; the nights did not have enough hours to satisfy my need for Edward."[37]

It is not surprising that Stephenie Meyer ends the final *Twilight* series book with a chapter titled "The Happily Ever After." As I said in Chapter One, good stories always move their "once upon a time" through a series of obstacles toward the eventual "happily ever after." We carry this expectation into every story we read, not because we want to escape reality—but because we want to connect with it. Christians know that the closing chapter of the story in which we believe includes Light overcoming darkness, Good conquering evil, and Prince Charming marrying Cinderella.

If you read through the entire Bible you will

discover that the most consistent and compelling image used to reveal the relationship between God and humanity is that of husband and wife. In the Old Testament, God is husband and Israel His adulterous wife.

> *"I remember the devotion of your youth, how as a bride you loved me and followed me through the desert...But you have lived as a prostitute with many lovers...Return, faithless people,"* declares the Lord, *"for I am your husband. I will choose you..."* (Jeremiah 2:2; 3:1,14 NIV).

In the New Testament, Christ is the Bridegroom and the Church His Bride.

> *For this reason a man will leave his father and mother and be united to his wife, and the two will become one flesh. This is a profound mystery—but I am talking about Christ and the church* (Ephesians 5:31-32 NIV).

I should once again note a difference between my Christian beliefs and those of Meyer's Mormon faith on this point. Christianity views marriage as an icon or analogy of the eternal union between God and humanity. Sorting out the beliefs of Mormons can be confusing because they use many of the same words but with very different meanings. One clear difference, however, relates to how marriage influences the destiny of the soul. Those who take part in "celestial marriage" by getting married in a Mormon temple, it is taught, can eventually have their own planet where they can continue to procreate spirit children for all eternity. The reason Mormons use the popular slogan "Family is forever" is because the church teaches that faithful couples can enter the "heaven" of their own godhood where they and their children can become actual deities.

Orthodox Christianity affirms the joy-filled marriage and family as the closest thing to Heaven we can experience in this life. But it recognizes them as mysterious icons of the real thing rather than as literal replacements for our coming union with the one and only God in the kingdom of Heaven when each man and woman who has accepted God's proposal becomes His eternal Bride.

The last chapter of the *Twilight* series is called *The Happily Ever After*. The final book of the Bible describes our happily ever after when the honeymoon of eternity begins.

"Hallelujah! For our Lord God Almighty reigns. Let us rejoice and be glad and give Him glory! For the wedding of the Lamb has come, and His bride has made herself ready. Fine linen, bright and clean, was given her to wear... I saw the Holy City, the new Jerusalem, coming down out of heaven from God, prepared as a bride beautifully dressed for her husband. And I heard a loud voice from the throne saying, "Now the dwelling of God is with men, and He will live with them. They will be His people, and God Himself will be with them and be their God. He will wipe every tear from their eyes. There will be no more death or mourning or crying or pain, for the old order of things has passed away" (Revelation 19:6-8; 21:2-4 NIV).

As we've discovered throughout this book, the *Twilight* phenomenon is nothing new. It is merely the most recent fairy tale to sweep us away into other worlds that can point us to profound truths resident in our real world. A story that confronts fans with the same question Edward and Bella encountered. What is the soul's destiny?

How we answer that question depends upon what larger, transcendent story frames and explains the scenes of our lives. Christians see the true story in which we live as a passionate love story, a fantastic adventure, and a suspenseful mystery. Author Frederick Buechner described it as tragedy, comedy, and fairy tale. It is first a tragedy because we encounter heartbreak, pain, and sorrow. It is also a comedy because the ending is one of joy and redemption. And it is fairy tale. In his words...

> *That is the Gospel, this meeting of darkness and light and the final victory of light. That is the fairy tale of the Gospel with, of course, the one crucial difference from all other fairy tales, which is that the claim made for it is that it is true, that it not only happened once upon a time but has kept happening ever since and is happening still.*[38]

As you bump into reminders of the true story of God in the scenes of *Twilight* or any other fantasy series, my prayer is that your eyes remain open to the wonderful place where life and story merge, and that your soul's *once upon a time* will discover the ultimate *happily ever after* for which it was made.

Conclusion

Questions and Answers

I have enjoyed watching the reaction of people who learn I have been writing a book about the *Twilight Phenomenon*. Most have at least heard of the series or seen trailers for the first movie, and each fall into one of three categories.

Younger fans (usually teen girls) light up—freely acknowledging that they luuuuuv the *Twilight* stories.

Older fans (usually moms) blush—a bit embarrassed to admit they too have devoured the books, almost as if I had caught them watching soap operas or purchasing trashy romance novels.

Non-fans (usually dads) scratch their heads—

curious why I would ask people to view the series through the lenses of Christian faith.

Those familiar with my earlier books exploring themes in popular stories such as *The Lord of the Rings*, *The Chronicles of Narnia*, *The Golden Compass*, and other fantasy tales ask whether I found anything at all redeeming about these vampire love stories.

As the preceding chapters have shown, the *Twilight* series does indeed raise important questions and touches upon profoundly spiritual themes. Let's take a moment to review and briefly address some of the major ones.

❧

Question: Would you describe the *Twilight* Series as a spiritual allegory?

Answer: No, I wouldn't. Allegory is a specific genre of literature where the author intentionally creates characters and scenes to portray some deeper truth or lesson. John Bunyan's classic book *Pilgrim's Progress* would be a good example, where every character is meant to represent something else and where the story arc is merely an excuse for teaching Christian theology. Fantasy literature, by contrast, is about telling a great story that may evoke important themes—but only by nature of the fact all great stories follow the same basic pattern of good vs. evil, romance, adventure, and heroics. Fantasy tales, whether they feature vampires or hobbits, carry us off into a world with rules different from our own—a world often governed by magic or some other fantastic elements. Yes, the *Twilight* series touches spiritual themes and implies a certain faith perspective. But it is not an intentionally crafted religious allegory. This book has tried to decipher the inference of Stephenie Meyer's imagination, not reveal her conscious agenda.

❧

Question: What does the *Twilight* series suggest about the nature of the soul?

Answer: As I tried to explain in Chapter Six, Stephenie Meyer's view of the soul and its destiny surfaces throughout the four books. Edward has what Bella considers an old-fashioned belief and value system. He wonders whether vampires even have souls, and if they do whether that soul is hopelessly damned. He holds on to the slight possibility that remaining sexually chaste until marriage will give him a shot at redemption—even though he has violated most of the remaining Ten Commandments. Bella comes across as a skeptic—dismissing Edward's concern over the destiny of his or her soul. But neither can escape the "rules" Meyer has created for their world. In Meyer's theology, the ultimate destiny of the soul is celestial marriage with ultimate godhood attained through self-disciplined obedience. Christians believe the soul is destined for eternal life by trusting in the sacrifice of Jesus Christ. (See John 3:16.) Mormons, in contrast, believe the soul is destined for godhood by following in the footsteps of Jesus Christ. (See *So What's the Difference* by Fritz Ridenour, Chapter Ten.)

Question: Do you consider Bella an admirable character?

Answer: Girls seem to admire *Twilight's* protagonist as a girl with an independent spirit who knows what she wants and refuses to follow anyone else's rules. Bella lies to nearly everybody to get her way. She also seems a bit arrogant, distancing herself from the teenage world of her friends because she prefers romancing the dangerous bad-boy to hanging out with "immature" high school guys.

As a Spiritual Formation Pastor, I find these qualities troubling because they run counter to what it means to be a Christ-like woman who walks in humility and grace. Frankly, Bella is a difficult character to like throughout much of the series because she is self-consumed, manipulative, deceptive, and moody. Who wants to hang out with a girl who seems apathetic or gloomy half of the time? She lacks many of the qualities historically associated with femininity—including an upbeat, nurturing spirit that makes a girl appealing to boys. Until forced, Bella is even averse to the joys of marriage and motherhood. It seems the primary reason boys like her is because she is physically attractive. And while beauty is a good thing worthy of attention, it is also vain and fleeting.

❧

Question: What do the *Twilight* vampires suggest about the spirit world?

Answer: Stephenie Meyer seems to have created a new breed of vampire very different from the monsters found in gothic horror. They share a thirst for human blood and possess tremendous physical strength. But they differ in many, many ways. Rather than monsters fallen from their once exalted state as human beings made in the image of God, Meyer's vampires seem more like super heroes or super villains. They are not the condemned, undead creatures of folklore. They are instead those who have attained supernatural status.

From a religious perspective, they actually remind us more of ancient paganism than biblical Christianity. In the spirit of Greek and Roman mythology, Meyer's supernatural characters behave very much like gods who either manipulate and destroy human beings (like Neptune and Hades) or intervene to protect them (like Athena and Artemis). The "god" Edward and human Bella even echo the ancient myth of Hercules by conceiving a "demigod" child—one who is a cross-breed between an immortal god and mortal human being. One of the Vladimir villain vampires even described himself as one who had been contemplating "our own divinity" as they "thought ourselves gods."[1] Traditional vampire stories grew up in a world that believed in the reality of demonic forces who could overtake human will and destroy human life as part of their rebellion against the creator of life. Meyer's stories are more like superhero tales rooted in religious polytheism.

Question: Does Jacob's character carry any spiritual significance?

Answer: The love triangle between Bella, Edward, and Jacob makes these books page-turners. Readers find themselves rooting for Jacob as he pursues Bella's heart because he is such a nice guy who is easy to like. In fact, I consider Jacob to be the most consistently heroic character throughout the *Twilight* series because he repeatedly lays aside his own desires in order to do what's best for Bella. He also manages to awaken within her a spark of life you don't find in her relationship with Edward. At one point Bella admits that she feels "much, much healthier around Jacob."[2] The Bible describes it as iron sharpening iron—one person helping make another person better. In that sense, Jacob is a very positive character who reminds us of the grace of friendship.

❧

Question: What is the underlying message we can take from the *Twilight Phenomenon?*

Answer: Every story reflects some spiritual perspective—whether it intends to do so or not. To decipher the overarching message of the *Twi-*

light series we need to consider the three worldview questions I mentioned in Chapter Two.

- **Question #1: What are we made for?** Human beings are made for more than meets the eye. Bella Swan spends much of the series disconnected from the larger purpose of her existence. She seems apathetic and passive because she is cut off from that which can give her passionate meaning. She mocks Edward for his old-fashioned beliefs, but can't suppress the desire to discover a larger meaning to her life.

- **Question #2: What is wrong with our world?** There are many things wrong in Bella's world. Her parents are divorced. Her mom seems flighty, her dad disengaged. Bella encounters an epic battle between good vampires and evil monsters hungry to devour human life. But the real drama of her story is not about surviving the blood lust of vampires. It is about satisfying an unrelenting desire for intimacy. Put simply, Bella has isolated herself from others and, in the process, cut herself off from life as intended.

- **Question #3: How will it be made right?** In the world created by Stephenie Meyer, Bella's dilemma is solved when she finally discovers the supernatural purpose for which she was created. Reading the scenes from her first moments as a mother (and as a vampire) imply a boundless happiness and anticipate an eternal intimacy. She describes her "happily ever after" in terms every person would love to find. "The life I'd fought for was safe again. My family was reunited. My daughter had a beautiful future stretching out endlessly in front of her...But most significant in this tidal wave of happiness was the surest fact of all: I was with Edward. Forever."[3]

Each of us, like Bella Swan, is haunted by an unrelenting desire for intimacy. We get a taste of our ultimate purpose when we fall in love with that special someone. But someday those who accept His invitation will find their way home into the arms of the God who made us for eternal relationship with Himself.

So, should we view the *Twilight Phenomenon* as thirst-quenching fantasy or forbidden fruit? Clearly, it contains elements of both. As a devout Christian, I disagree when hints of Stephenie Meyer's theology pushes its way into her stories. But that is to be expected of any writer. As a pastor and father, I find it troubling that so many young girls are devouring books with themes inappropriate for their age. But as a theologian and fantasy literature enthusiast, I consider the *Twilight Phenomenon* an ideal opportunity to collectively explore the "true myth" that lies beneath every great story.

Endnotes

Introduction

1.   Lev Grossman, "Stephenie Meyer: A New J.K. Rowling?" April 24, 2008; http://www.time.com/time/magazine/article/0,9171,1734838,00.html

Chapter 1

1.   Stephenie Meyer, *Breaking Dawn* (New York: Little, Brown and Company, 2008), 479.

2.   Paul Harvey, radio and newspaper commentary.

3.   Ibid.

4. J.R.R. Tolkien, *The Tolkien Reader* (New York: Ballantine Books, 1966) 79

CHAPTER 2

1. *Breaking Dawn*, 525.

2. C.S. Lewis, *God in the Dock* (Grand Rapids: Eerdmanns Publishing Company, 1970), 66-67.

3. J.R.R. Tolkien, *The Tolkien Reader* (New York: Del Ray, 1986), 71-72.

4. Dorothy Sayers, *The Man Born to be King* (London: Victor Gollancz, Ltd., 1943), 20.

5. David Downing, *The Most Reluctant Convert: C.S. Lewis' Journey to Faith* (Downers Grove, IL: InterVarsity Press, 2002), II.

6. Ibid.

7. C.S. Lewis, *Of Other Worlds* (San Diego: Harcourt Brace Jovanovich, 1966), 36.

8. Lyle W. Dorsett and Marjorie Lamp Mead, eds., *C.S. Lewis: Letters to Children* (New York: Scribner, 1996).

9. C.S. Lewis, *Mere Christianity* (New York: Simon & Schuster, 1996), 121.

CHAPTER 3

1. *Breaking Dawn*, 302.

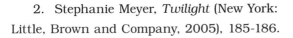
2. Stephanie Meyer, *Twilight* (New York: Little, Brown and Company, 2005), 185-186.

3. Michelle Belanger, *Vampires in Their Own Words* (Woodbury, MN: Llewellyn Publications, 2007), xiii.

4. Random House Dictionary Online, 2009; http://dictionary.reference.com/browse/vampirism.

5. Merriam-Webster's Medical Dictionary, 2002; http://dictionary.reference.com/browse/vampirism.

6. The following overview is gratefully derived from a much more comprehensive collection of vampire lore assembled by Rosemary Ellen Guiley's *Encyclopedia of Vampires, Werewolves, and Other Monsters* (New York: Checkmark Books, 2005).

7. Ibid., 3.

8. Ibid., 51.

9. Ibid., 116.

10. Ibid., 152.

11. Ibid., 118.

12. Ibid., 141.

13. Belanger, xiii.

14. Guiley, 28.

15. Ibid., 257.

16. Ibid., 133.

17. Anne Rice, *Interview with the Vampire* (New York: Ballantine Books, 1976), 163.

18. Wikipedia article at: http://en.wikipedia.org/wiki/The_Vampyre#cite_note-0.

19. Ibid.

20. Guiley, 108.

21. Bram Stoker, *Dracula* (New York, Bantam Books, 1989), 200.

22. Ibid., 157.

23. Ibid., 339.

24. Ibid., 362.

25. Wikipedia; http://en.wikipedia.org/wiki/I_Am_Legend.

26. Rice.

27. Summarized from Wikipedia article; http://en.wikipedia.org/wiki/Vlad_III_the_Impaler.

28. Summarized from Wikipedia; http://en.wikipedia.org/wiki/Erzs%C3 %A9bet_B%C3%A1thory. Additional details from Guiley, 20-21.

29. Summarized from Wikipedia; http://

en.wikipedia.org/wiki/Fritz_Haarmann.
Additional details from Guiley, 143.

   30. Wikipedia; http://en.wikipedia.org/wiki/
John_George_Haigh. Additional details from
Guiley, 144.

   31. http://www.lyricsdrive.com/lyrics/
macabre/430639/acid-bath-vampire-john
-george-haigh-lyrics/.

CHAPTER 4

   1. *Twilight*, 195.

   2. Lewis, *Mere Christianity*, 121.

   3. Nicene Constantinopolitan Creed 381.

   4. *Catechism of the Catholic Church* (Second
Edition) # 2205, 589.

   5. Ibid., #2361, 626.

   6. *Twilight*, 19.

   7. Ibid., 206.

   8. Ibid., 256.

   9. St. Thomas Aquinas, *The Pocket Aquinas*
(New York: Pocket Books, 1960), 269.

   10. Genesis 1:27.

   11. *Twilight*, 303.

12. Philippians 2:8.

13. *Twilight,* 180.

14. Christopher West, *The Theology of the Body for Beginners* (West Chester, PA: Ascension Press, 2004), 121-122).

Chapter 5

1. Lev Grossman, "Stephenie Meyer: A New J.K. Rowling?", *Time*; http://www.time .com/time/magazine/article/0,9171,1734838,00 .html; accessed (June 4, 2009).

2. *Twilight,* 218-230.

3. Ibid., 264-282.

4. Ibid., 298-311.

5. Stephenie Meyer, *New Moon* (New York: Little, Brown and Company, 2006), 50-52.

6. Ibid., 512.

7. Stephenie Meyer, *Eclipse* (New York: Little, Brown and Company, 2007), 43-44.

8. Ibid., 186-188.

9. Ibid., 324.

10. Ibid., 437-452.

11. *New Moon,* 540-541.

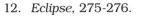

12. *Eclipse*, 275-276.

13. *Eclipse*, 443-456.

14. C.S. Lewis, *Screwtape Letters* (New York: Bantam Books, 1982), 26.

15. C.S. Lewis, *The Weight of Glory* (San Francisco: Harper San Francisco, 1980), 26.

16. Ibid., 25.

17. *Catechism*, 447.

18. *Book of Common Prayer*, 300.

CHAPTER 6

1. *Twilight*, 87.

2. Ibid., 270.

3. Ibid., 342-343.

4. *New Moon*, 546.

5. Ibid., 69.

6. Stephenie Meyer, *Breaking Dawn* (New York: Little, Brown and Company, 2008), 24.

7. *Eclipse*, 273.

8. Ibid., 453-455.

9. *Twilight*, 135.

10. *Eclipse*, 620.

11. *Twilight*, 87.

12. *Eclipse*, 25-26.

13. *Twilight*, 184.

14. Ibid., 187.

15. *Eclipse*, 300.

16. Ibid., 329.

17. Ibid., 421.

18. *Twilight*, 336-339.

19. Ibid., 204.

20. *Breaking Dawn*, 466.

21. *Twilight*, 306-307.

22. Ibid., 301.

23. Romans 7:18.

24. Romans 7:24–8:4.

25. Romans 6:23.

26. Romans 5:8.

27. 1 Peter 5:8.

28. Fritz Ridenour, *So What's the Difference?* (Ventura: Regal Publishers, 2001), 145.

29. Ibid., 145.

30. *Breaking Dawn*, 6.

31. Ibid., 133.

32. Ibid., 132.

33. Ibid., 374-378

34. Ibid., 446-447.

35. Ibid., 524.

36. Ibid., 483.

37. Ibid., 527.

38. Frederick Buechner, *Telling the Truth* (New York: HarperCollins, 1977), 90.

Conclusion

1. *Breaking Dawn,* 631.

2. *New Moon,* 159.

3. *Breaking Dawn,* 751-752.

OTHER BOOKS BY
KURT BRUNER

Finding God in the Lord of the Rings

Finding God in the Land of Narnia

Inklings of God

I Still Believe

The Divine Drama

Shedding Light on His Dark Materials

Your Heritage

How to Mess Up Your Child's Life

Playstation Nation

❧

For free downloadable resources to help you go
further in your spiritual journey visit

www.KurtBruner.com

About the Author

❧

KURT BRUNER is a best-selling author of books that explore the common thread of morality in pop culture, including *Finding God in the Lord of the Rings, Shedding Light on His Dark Materials, Playstation Nation, Finding God in the Land of Narnia,* and How to Mess Up Your Child's Life.

Additional copies of this book and other book titles from DESTINY IMAGE are available at your local bookstore.

Call toll-free: 1-800-722-6774.

Send a request for a catalog to:

Destiny Image® Publishers, Inc.
P.O. Box 310
Shippensburg, PA 17257-0310

*"Speaking to the Purposes of God for This
Generation and for the Generations to Come."*

**For a complete list of our titles,
visit us at www.destinyimage.com.**